BEYOND THE MISTS OF TIME

WHEN TREES RULED THE EARTH AND THE STATE OF BALANCE AND EUPHORIA THAT ENSUED THERE FROM

BY

Robert J. Newton, J.D., N.D

To Shirley

Aleph Kaf Aleph

(restoring things to their
perfect state)

10-2-16

BEYOND THE MISTS OF TIME

ADVANCE PRAISE

I am a homeopathic doctor who has specialized in using homeopathic remedies to make plants grow faster and healthier. I was pleasantly surprised just how insightful Dr. Newton's *Beyond the Mists of Time*, and I found it very readable and compelling, just like his previous books, *The Hidden Codes of God*, *A Map to Healing...* and *Pathways to God*. This new book manages to top *The Hidden Codes of God*, which is also completely engrossing. I read many parts of *Beyond the Mists of Time* to my granddaughter and she was also very engrossed by the book. Readers will find this book takes horticulture, botany and archaeology into new territory while telling a fascinating story; it also tells us how we can create heaven on Earth."

~ **Dr. Vaikunthanath Kaviraj**

"This book gave me a new perspective on so many things, but especially very old cultures that virtually no one knows anything about. I am most grateful to Dr. Newton for sharing a story that just wraps you up in it and makes you want to read more and more! *Beyond the Mists of Time* is a worthy successor to Dr. Newton's *The Hidden Codes of God*. One thing I like about Dr. Newton's novels is that you are entertained and also learning many things, concurrently. Beyond that, Doc manages to give insights and solutions to many problems facing humanity at this time. Everyone should read this book!"

~ **Thomas Morton, CEO**
Light Speed Learning

v

Beyond the Bounds of Earth Publishing, Entertainment and Education

Great Motivational Talks
ISBN-13: 978-0996137126
ISBN-10: 0996137122

Dr. Robert J. Newton
20253 Evening Breeze Dr.
Walnut, California 91789

http://www.drrobertnewton.com/

Ordering Information:
Quantity sales. Special discounts are available on quantity purchases by corporations, associations, and others. For details, contact the publisher at the address above.

Printed in the United States of America

First Edition

14 13 12 11 10 / 10 9 8 7 6 5 4 3 2 1

DEDICATION

This book is dedicated to those people with such an intense thirst to know and understand God they will overcome any obstacle put in their path of this pursuit. Always question everything; yet be pliable enough to accept new information that might be contrary to what you have already learned. At the very least, if you cannot understand something when it is presented to you, suspend judgment until you can ascertain the accuracy thereof. Also, never be reticent to ask for scientific and annotated proof of what someone presented to you, especially those who ask you to accept something on "blind belief." Additionally, know as certitude you can accomplish anything when you put your thoughts, energy, and powers of visualization toward accomplishing your goal. Live by this maxim, "The fool didn't know it couldn't be done, so it went ahead and did it anyway" (unknown). If you really want to get deeply into the concepts found throughout this book, check my other books including: *A Map to Healing and Your Essential Divinity Through Theta Consciousness, Pathways to God: Experiencing the Energies of the Living God in Your Everyday Life* and *The Hidden Codes of God.*

Namaste, Dr. Newton

TABLE OF CONTENTS

PREFACE

As do my other books, including *Pathways to God: Experiencing the Energies of the Living God in Your Everyday Life*, *A Map to Healing and Your Essential Divinity Through Theta Consciousness*, and *The Hidden Codes of God*, this new book, *Beyond the Mists of Time* kind of takes on a life of its own. I know roughly where I am going with the story but allow myself to be led as my intuition directs me. I have spent considerable time studying the prehistoric cultures of Lemuria/Mu and Atlantis but there is scant information about these cultures; we do have some references to Atlantis by Plato, Sophocles and Herodotus. There is some evidence that this country existed, since all of these figures are known for their integrity and vast understanding of things. There are also megalithic ruins in various parts of the Atlantic Ocean, which are most likely related to Atlantis. Possibly the records necessary to verify the existence of Lemuria are submerged with other records of the Atlantean civilization. The venerated Rudolph Steiner wrote *Atlantis and Lemuria,* yet my accounts of those civilizations are different. The variance can be explained by different timelines accounted for in Quantum Mechanics of the various parallel Earth dimensions.

With a blank slate, and no preconceptions, I also spent a lot of time studying the Egyptian temples and pyramids after I went to Egypt in 1984. The experiences I had inside the temples and pyramids were so profound they still affect me to this day, in a very positive way, especially as it relates to opening my psychic abilities and learning the amazing things that happen when we employ these God given gifts. Egypt is our closest civilization to Atlantis and Lemuria and my intuition submits both the Atlanteans and Lemurians were intricately involved in the amazing structures that are extant in Egypt today, as well as the Sumerians from the planet, Nibiru, and a civilization from the planet, Sirius B, since there is a shaft in the Great Pyramid in Giza aligned directly thereto.

When the continent of Atlantis started splitting and subducting, there was an exodus of citizens not only to Egypt but also to Central America and South America. We find links in the personage of Hermes/Thoth/Enoch, who wound up in the Mayan civilization as Quetzalcoatl, and who was Thoth in Egypt and Sumeria… and Enoch in Palestine. Additionally we have the multi-ton corner stones in The Temple of the Sphinx in Giza, Egypt and a temple in Machu Picchu, Peru. It is through these synchronicities that we obtain supportive evidence, which allows us to see just how much interaction there was between the pre-historic and historic cultures discussed herein.

Many people have proposed that extra terrestrials were the genesis of the cultures and the megalithic temples and pyramids that we have on Earth today. This is easier to accept when you realize the Sumerian's/Anunaki came from Nibiru, a distant planet on an elliptical orbit in our solar system. Please check Zecharia Sitchin's 10 books used for the research regarding this topic, including *The Lost Realms*. Additionally, we found plans for a very advanced spacecraft engine/propulsion system in *The Vedas* from the Hindu tradition in India.

This could in fact indicate an ET connection since there are descriptions of aircraft in *The Mahābhārata* and *The Ramayana*, two great Indian epics that describe the kind of aircraft that does not exist today, except at Area 51 at the Groom Lake, Nevada, Air Force Base. It is further known that Hitler directed his scientists to peruse *The Vedas*, which you might otherwise recognize as a great body of works that is known to form the oldest collective of Sanskrit literature, as his country researched and created a German flying saucer!

It seems that these prehistoric and historic civilizations functioned at a very high level with virtually no sickness or disease and unlimited liberty for the citizens of these various cultures… until they started drifting away from a very close connection to Nature. They also had very long lifetimes extending into hundreds of years and more! Once this connection became compromised, sickness and disease became prolific and liberty for the citizens of Earth started disappearing.

So what I saw from reviewing all the civilizations you see covered in this book was: We can take the best of what they manifested and apply it to our own problems today to create a Heaven on Earth. Granted, there are epidemics of sickness and disease today and undeniably virtually every government on Earth is doing everything in their power to control their citizens, thereby squelching our liberty. Allow yourself to drift into the stories of the ancient civilizations and then see how we can restore things to their perfect state as per the 7th Name of God from "Exodus" 14, 19-21 of *The Torah*, Aleph Kaf Aleph!

ACKNOWLEDGEMENTS

Dr. Newton acknowledges the amazing teachers who helped him further his quest for spiritual knowledge and understanding of romantic and Divine Love. Those teachers include, John Alfred Clark, Edith Anderson, Mary Jane Heitzman, Julio Rivas, Mary Baker Eddy, Robert Chuck Schwartz, Charlette Ann Newton Smith, Dr. Paul Spin, Patrice Rybicki, Pamela Parvati Thomas, Yogi Govindan Satchidananda, Tim Latimer, Thomas Morton, William Sink, Babaji Nagaraj, Satchi Sai Baba, Amachi, Sri Aurobindo, Ghandi, Neem Karoli Baba, Paramahansa Yoganada, Yogi S.A.A. Ramaiah, Krishna, Yeshua (Jesus), Dr. Paul Foster Case, Hermes Trismegistus, Asclepias, Vianna Stibal, Louise L. Hay, Dr. James J. Hurtak, Dr. Wayne Dyer, Dr. Fred Bell, Ervin Lazlo, Rudolph Steiner, Ken Keyes, David Wilcock, Valery P. Kondratov, Gurudeva, Dr. Hugh Ross, Louis Contant, Dr. Rocco Erico, Rev. Richard Hill, and William Henry. Learn from these people in person, via their books, or their energy presence… you will rarely be misled!

| CHAPTER ONE

GENESIS, THE REAL BEGINNING AND THE NATURE OF THINGS, AS IT WERE!

James, having finished writing his book, *The Hidden Codes of God,* with Dr. Robert Newton, experienced strong feelings the solutions for all the ills of society was contained within the laws of Nature and Natural Law and the ancient civilizations that embraced and understood these things. He had learned techniques for past life regression and possessed a finely honed array of psychic abilities, including remote viewing, and realized that most of the information he needed to uncover would not come from books.

Knowing the process of "looking into/viewing" the past, a part of remote viewing, would certainly be crucial to his quest; James often used remote viewing to see/view into future timelines/events, but the task called for him to visit the old timelines, which were apart of unrecorded and lost historical records… such as what happened in Atlantis.

Although there are shards of evidence that a very advanced civilization, known as Atlantis, is believed by some people to be a reality, including the genius mind of Rudolf Steiner, many people, especially archaeologists, believe the existence of Atlantis is sheer speculation. Plato, Aristotle and Sophocles talked about the Atlantean civilization, as did "The Sleeping Prophet," Edgar Cayce. Theosophist luminaries such as C.S. Ledbetter, Madame Blavatsky and Anne Besant also shared information about Atlantis and Lemuria/Mu that was not contained in any books or records at the time of their revelations. Even the singer, Donovan, wrote and performed a song about Atlantis. The pop-song, which was written and recorded by a British singer/songwriter, was a popular single released in 1968; it has not been forgotten!

Beyond and predating all of this, Swami Saraswati, in *The True History and Religion of India*, traced the genesis of the Indian culture back 1.9 billion years. His calculations were supported by studying ancient Indian texts, including the Vedas and Upanishads… counting backwards, and using the several hundred thousand time spans of the Yugas (four recurring cycles of time). Even with this as a background, James knew he would need to use his myriad abilities to write a definitive book about the beginnings of the history of Earth.

Through practicing Kriya Kundalini Pranayam, a secret and extended breathing technique from Kriya Kundalini Yoga, his consciousness entered altered brainwave levels of Alpha, Theta and even Delta. This level of consciousness would serve James well as he plowed eagerly into the task he was so anxious to undertake. These are the brainwave levels normally met in hypnosis and even beyond… wherein amazing insights and creativity are revealed to those who know how to enter the realms in theta consciousness! In fact, James experienced these abilities through his assiduous meditation practices from Tai Chi and Kriya Kundalini Yoga!

So after performing about a half an hour of Kriya Kundalini Pranayam breathing, James knew he was at an enhanced level of Theta/Delta consciousness, which would allow him to access information that was called "Akashic knowledge" in the Indian *Vedas* and *Upanishads* and known as "Celestial knowledge" in The *Yoga Sutras,* by Sat guru-Avatar, Patañjali.

While James remained in this trance state consciousness, which some people have compared to be like being in a dream, yet others describe as an enhanced or deeper state of perception, many amazing things were revealed to him that he shared in his book. James was aware he had entered the altered brainwave state; he was almost asleep, yet still awake. Another indicator of enhanced levels of consciousness was James being in Samadhi, a condition where his breathing and heart functions ceased, and he was in a "near death" experience. James would always enter this Samadhi state after long sessions of Pranayam breathing meditation and during extended periods throughout periods of everyday life.

As James began his remote viewing session in Samadhi, he was prepared to see things like nothing he had seen or known before and what he was about to behold was more than he could have ever imagined! The first of many things James saw was the beginning of planet Earth, previously known as Gaia, during a time frame that was billions of years ago—possibly even more—at a time before any people or extra terrestrial civilizations had visited or inhabited the beautiful planet, Gaia. James had the privilege to view Gaia/Earth as lushly covered with innumerable plant forms and abundantly populated with many types of animal and fish forms, both on the land and the sea.

But the most magnificent views, including plant forms or animals and fish, were of the many varied species of trees. Many of these trees reached a stature of magnificence such as redwood trees, with canopies that reached even higher than many of today's tallest skyscrapers. There were also smaller trees like alder and birch and a lot of small understory plants. The most prolific of these plants were innumerable groups of various fern plants at a time when lushness pervaded much of the land on Earth. The best comparison of this James could see was the present place of Muir Woods, just north of San Francisco, California. A beautiful National Monument tucked into nature and runs along the Pacific coast, it comprises over 200 acres of amazing redwoods.

It was clearly revealed to James that there were at least three reasons for the incredible size of the trees… one was that very high oxygen content existed in the atmosphere on this planet, which at this time was synthesized by the roots of the trees and plants. Another reason for the exorbitant growth of some of these trees was that the Sun was brighter and produced hotter temperatures, fomenting an ideal growing environment. This reality was in direct contravention to the accepted notion of our time that too much Sun or heat is viewed as a deterrent to optimum plant growth. The third reason for the unbridled growth of many of the trees was the huge amounts of rain, saturated with hydrogen peroxide, infused with many atoms of oxygen, is a tremendous growth accelerator for plants and trees.

The common thread among these three growth factors is that all of these things intensified the life force energies of the Creator, which are electromagnetic in effect and also include scalar waves, often referred to as Prana/Chi/life force or electromagnetic energy, but not limited thereto. The oxygen factors of the atmosphere and the hydrogen peroxide created an optimum factor for energy, the oxygen actually being a mode that readily transmitted and transferred vastly higher amounts of Prana/Chi that could be utilized by the trees and plants! The accelerated effects could have also been due to the hydrogen in the atmosphere, as well, because it is also a carrier agent of Prana/Chi. Either way, it was the bonding of the Prana to the oxygen and hydrogen that made plants and trees grow faster.

The light factors of the Sun were also obviously growth enhancers likewise and referred to as in such texts such as *The Bhagavad Gita*. Again, this sunlight was infused with vast amounts of Prana… the result of the explosion of hydrogen gas and a little helium within the Sun itself. The accumulation of enhancers caused the trees and plants to proliferate and thrive beyond anything people of this time have ever known. It was similar to the growth rates prevalent in our jungles today, but at a rate and force of squaring or even cubing what happens in the best growing environments of our present time. There were no developed civilizations, or the air pollution or electromagnetic wave pollution there from, to dilute this high oxygen and Prana saturation!

Even though the extremely tall trees created a dense canopy that only allowed filtered Sun to reach the understory trees and plants, these smaller plants were still able to thrive and adapted to conditions of lesser light factors which were oftentimes dense shade. But unlike humans today, even though the trees and plants competed for the same soil nutrients, oxygen and Sun, all of the trees and plant forms had an intuitive understanding that there were enough of the common things they needed to survive… and even prosper!

And there was a mutual understanding that all the plants and trees and animals were interconnected through the same field of energy that had been manifested by the Creator. So James could see herein, that indeed humans could learn how to live harmoniously with each other by following the templates of cooperation inherently expressed in Nature.

Since all tree and plant forms understood all their needs would be met… fear, anger and resentment were unknown among them; nor were competition, grudges and wars. Even the gargantuan trees felt no need to take and hoard more nutrients than they required for their immediate needs. So without the scarcity mentality, the larger trees allowed the smaller trees and plants to live, even though they could have easily assimilated all of the nutrients and resources, which would have caused the other plants to slowly wither and die.

There was actually a symbiosis where the various plants shared factors that they had in excess, such as iron, nitrogen, phosphorous, potassium, and other minerals. Furthermore, the larger trees did not use their superior mass to try and dominate or control the smaller plant forms. All of these things made factual sense to James, because of his extensive background and experience in horticulture!

Interestingly, the large trees also had fractal/proportional geometries in the amounts of their branches that had a direct relationship to the number of smaller trees. It was necessary, this fractal geometric relationship, so there would be adequate numbers of trees to absorb enough carbon dioxide to keep the atmosphere is a good balance… a state of symbiosis, where oxygen existed in enormous amounts. Indeed, only a great cosmic intelligence/Creator/God would be so prescient as to create such a complete template/plan of life to ensure there would be perpetual sustainability in nature!

There was also a direct fractal proportional relationship among the amount of branches and roots that was part of the trees' structural design. Such an insight was something James had never previously considered in the realm of possibilities, but the relationships certainly showed a recurring pattern of "intelligent design" within Nature, as opposed to randomness or chaos.

James was quite familiar with the process wherein a legume type plant produced excess nitrogen, which it then shared with neighboring trees and plants. If other plants could more easily extract phosphorous and potassium from the soil, the excess beyond their needs could be released and shared with other trees and plants. When the large trees began to attract and multiply mychorhizzae fungus around their roots, it proliferated and spread to the smaller trees and plants, which then helped them absorb a higher level of nutrients. Additionally, animal manures nourished the trees with ammonium nitrite; as the leaves from the trees and plants decomposed, nitrate nitrogen, easily absorbable by the plants and trees, was released.

There was no need for a governmental structure in this natural environment, since peace and order prevailed and all tree and plant forms thrived without such stifling, pernicious and inherently ineffective organizational structures, which people today embrace and think are an essential part of civilization! James was ardent in sharing his perception that this inter-sharing of resources was most assuredly a key to the

balance and sustainability of nature and its components…
and necessary for human civilization likewise.

This meant likewise that trees and plants and animals
only occupied as much land as they needed and there were no
species that hoarded and occupied things beyond their
immediate needs! From James' perspective, as he viewed the
elements of a natural environment, he could see the very
structure fully circumvented the greed factor that leads to
innumerable problems in today's societies. The nonexistence
of greed was founded on a lack of fear of the scarcity of
resources, which obviated the need or compulsion to possess
things in excess of what any species, or their family, could
reasonably use!

Even the numerous animal species lived in peace and
there was only killing when carnivores killed another species
so as to have nourishment. In most cases, killing for the
purpose of nourishment occurred on an-as-needed basis—
there was no genocide and no hoarding of food. Likewise, no
food source was wasted even though it was in plentiful
supply.

Some of the trees produced fruit for the herbivorous
animals and birds and, likewise, these herbivores often ate
leaves from the trees, but never so much as to cause stress or
harm to the trees. The animals that ate the fruits and leaves
would also eat insect infestations that could potentially
damage or kill the trees. They had an intuitive understanding
to not eat too many leaves and understood their food sources
would not last if the insect populations reached epidemic
proportions.

The animals also knew that they could not survive if the plants did not sequester carbon dioxide and clean the air of other naturally occurring pollution. And the animals and birds that ate the fruits helped propagate new trees as they excreted seeds in their manure from the fruits they had consumed. These manures then, enriched the structure of the soil so that it became more fertile and flocculated into a permeable state. So basically, what was created was something beyond a Garden of Eden scenario—a utopia on Gaia, so to speak—— that actually exceeded anything described in Genesis in *The Torah* or *The Holy Bible*. The interdependence of all life-beings was repeatedly being brought to James' attention.

James likewise saw that much of the same evidence of symbiosis occurred in the world's oceans. The fish and sea mammals—seals, dolphins and whales—know that each is interdependent on survival and cannot exist without being connected to even the lowliest forms of plankton. Planktons are consumed by all species and there is an inherent understanding of their importance. Granted, larger fish consume smaller fish, but everything is held in balance by this natural, intuitive understanding: if everything is consumed in moderation, there will always be an abundance of food to consume and the ocean's ecosystem will continue to produce a bounty that benefits all ocean creatures.

The manures from the fish sustain seaweed and kelp and even coral, which are also nitrified by ammonal nitrogen expelled from the gills of fish. And the corals reefs, in turn, give habitat and refuge to the fish, mammals and other sea creatures! As on land, prosperity reigns within the oceans because there remains a bounty for all and thus there is no need or thought to hoard food and nutrient resources! This makes the need for government, once again, unnecessary and perceived as obviously redundant!

Birds would consume fish as well as fruit, berries, grains and other seeds. But again, there was a symbiotic relationship where they nitrified sea plants with their manures. No animal or plant form ever "thought" of this symbiosis because it was the inherent and natural order of life already formed by the Creator, who manifested the order from an intelligent and holistic perspective. And so it was… and so it remained for many billions of years.

In his trance, several times James saw civilizations from other star systems that would come to explore and survey the bountiful creation on the Gaia. James could clearly see that he was involved in one of these expeditions in a previous lifetime on another planet, Sirius B. Since these civilizations had to travel long distances and needed advanced propulsion systems that allowed them to travel just below the speed of light, to even get to Earth, by and large, these explorers had a collective of expanded consciousness that comprehended the vibrancy of the forces of Nature in operation on Gaia! Thus they were careful not to intervene in the perfect order of things by leaving the smallest of imprints on the Earth during their visits.

But mining on Gaia was performed by extra-terrestrial civilizations, mostly from Sirius, as discussed in *The Sirius Mystery by* Robert Temple and Nibiru, discussed in Zecharia Sitchin's books like *When Time Began.* Mainly, what they concentrated on was the extraction of gold and silver. Gold was given special consideration; it has an octahedral form at the atomic level, and the uses of this precious metal were known to have rejuvenating properties within the body, similar to the monoatomic gold supplements like ormus… a precious metal in an exotic state of matter, where no bonds or crystal are formed and continue to exist as a separate single atom. These supplements are sold today and frequently used as a catalyst or accelerant used to expand the consciousness of an individual and aid in the attainment of the higher brainwaves, including Alpha, but more particularly Theta and Delta.

The gold was also used in electrical circuitry and for "zero-point energy" systems, which were perpetual energy generators of various types that did not require conventional fuel. It was also used to rebuild the depleted atmosphere on Nibiru, a planet in our solar system that was carelessly and stupidly destroyed, by over-industrialization and scientific atmospheric experiments gone awry. The destruction is akin to today's geo-engineering of the Earth's atmosphere, by aerosolizing the skies with chemicals, known as chemtrails! The miners also used the gold to regenerate their bodies, which was achieved by lengthening the telomerase strands of their DNA.

At times, fires were started by lightning that destroyed areas of the land. Usually the very tall trees, especially the redwood trees and oaks, would survive these fires. Whether these larger, stronger trees survived or not, much of the understory plants and trees were severely burned and often destroyed. Some of the plants and trees regenerated themselves from their roots, even though initially, they seemed to be completely dead. James marveled at the tenacity and prolific nature of these regenerating forces within the scheme of things, which revealed a system of Natural Law and Natural Regeneration. Of course, these forces remain evident today after wildfires decimate the plant forms from their fiery forces!

Regardless, such conflagrations allowed the smaller plants and trees to also regenerate from their seeds, which were made highly viable and ready to germinate into progeny from the plant forms that were killed, with the seeds, pods and cones that were left behind. The fires would cause the pods and cones to explode and dispense their seeds to the surrounding areas. Then eventually, as the new trees grew to larger heights, they caused a change in the flora and fauna… and then caused the new, smaller plants to decline in numbers.

And yet these smaller plants were an indispensible link in the process of regeneration because they allowed a moisture condition to prevail so the new tree seeds could germinate, under the shade of their canopy. This continual state of moisture existing under the canopy of the plants was necessary to soften the outer shell of the seed so that the enzymes could be released that allowed a sprout to germinate from the seed and then root into the ground. This process applied particularly to such trees as pinon pines and junipers, which can take several years to germinate after a fire; they needed plants like sage bush to reestablish themselves and create the proper conditions of shade and continual moisture so the tree seeds could germinate. The same thing applied to juniper bushes and trees.

The trees and plants communicated with each other through their trunks and branches, leaves, and roots and the mycorrhizae fungus that extended from the roots! The contact was not reached through a spoken language, but rather through symbols and pictures transmitted through the electronic field of energy in the atmosphere that surrounded all creation. It was like a wireless circuit of communication, and akin to human telepathy; and well depicted in the movie, *Avatar.*

As though this were not amazing enough, James also viewed how animals likewise communicated—interspecies and intraspecies—in this same manner. And beyond this, communication occurred between the plant forms and the animals. So there was intra civilization/species and inter civilization/species interaction; all visitors considered Gaia to be a Lotus Paradise—a land of great fragrance, flowers, fruits, vegetables and yes, those magnificent trees!

Because of his extensive background in horticulture, landscaping, and organic farming, all of what James saw and learned in his trance made sense to him. His experience provided enough of a background and "seeded thoughts" in which to make sense of the information and pictures he accessed via *The Akashic Records* and the knowledge contained therein. Additionally James' understanding of chemistry, physics, and quantum physics/mechanics also made the pictures and information more comprehendible for him.

James sensed, while in his trance, that with the degree of all-encompassing beauty, unbounded growth, and abundant fruits and vegetable and animals, it was only a matter of time until people from other star systems would come and colonize Gaia! In the meantime, the trees would record all events that occurred on Gaia in their memories and would be witness to and have memory of the civilizations that would be coming to Gaia/Earth.

Within these memories would be held the approach man could take to extricate himself from the numerous messes, including many wars and numerous types of manmade pollution, which would be created on Earth. James and his wife, Ann, would in fact use this knowledge and energy of the trees so perfection could become re-realized, as per "Aleph Kaf Aleph," the 7th Name of God from Exodus in the *Torah*, which translated to returning things to their perfect state! Just how this was accomplished would be most ingenious, but the process would only be revealed after James ventured into and reviewed the records and knowledge of the ancient civilizations!

| CHAPTER TWO

THE COLONIZATION OF GAIA/EARTH

Indeed, colonization was on the immediate horizon for Gaia, as James saw during his next "remote viewing" session, but what he saw was far more than almost anyone would be prepared to see. As previously mentioned, during the preceding billions (or trillions) years Gaia was inhabited, there was broad exploration and surveys by visitors from other star systems. These were already highly developed civilizations from planets such as the Sirius planets: Sirius A and Sirius B in the Orion's Belt, the Andromeda System and the Pleiades, also known as the Seven Sisters. All but a few were populated with people with vast esoteric and spiritual knowledge and traditions, as well as great scientific knowledge and perpetual motion, energy propulsion, and distribution systems.

Sometime after this, there were mining operations on Earth performed by the Anunaki, from the planet Nibiru, a planet in our solar system. The Anunaki were consumed with mining gold. The gold used to replenish their depleted atmosphere, which was the result of severe pollution of many types. It included electrical pollution, which is rarely considered by most as a pollutant, and chemical aerosols sprayed into the atmosphere, such as the chemtrails believed to be sprayed today in our atmosphere today!

Because of the expanded consciousness and intelligence of these star beings, they understood that people must live sustainably and not destroy the facets and factors of Nature that surrounded them. However, the Anunaki, being from this solar system via the planet Nibiru, did not have a highly expanded consciousness; they were equipped only with high technology, which included zero point energy systems and advanced propulsion systems.

But with the star people, of whom James had done previous remote viewings, he discerned the forces of nature kept them emotionally balanced and spiritually enhanced. Additionally, these star people knew if they destroyed the surrounding features of nature, they would certainly destroy themselves and life for them would cease. From James' perspective, this was certainly a belief not well understood today.

This first civilization on Gaia, a.k.a. Earth, arrived roughly 1.9 billion years ago and was located in India, which was called Ananda at its inception and included the area of what are now India, Tibet and Nepal. Ananda was a Sanskrit word for bliss, or something closely related thereto; Sanskrit was the language of this civilization. Ananda had advanced propulsion systems for interstellar spacecraft and domestic energy systems as per Tesla technology. They also used cold fusion, geomagmatic heat exchange and magnetic levitation generators, which are akin to zero point energy systems or perpetual motion devices and technologies as well as nuclear energy systems. The civilization's greatest achievement was the advanced spiritual knowledge they brought with them. James literally observed this through an incarnation he had in the time frame he was viewing.

This spiritual knowledge the Anandan's collected in *The Vedas* and *The Upanishads*, and later in *The Ramayana*, and other advanced Yogic texts that were eventually dispensed in *Thirumandiram* by Sat guru/Avatar Thirumoolar. It was also found dispensed Sat guru/Avatar Patanjali in *The Yoga Sutras*, and much later in *The Bhagavad Gita* and *The Mahabharata*, which involved the travails of Krishna and Arjuna, in an epic battle against the forces of evil!

Inherent in the evolved spiritual knowledge and the Yogic practices that came with it, there was a common knowledge and connection among all individuals, which James relived as he regressed into a previous incarnation at this inception of Ananda. The connection came through the energies of Shiva, God, and was and is present within all things; it definitely included the constituents of Nature and is articulated as the concept of Pantheism, today.

So, to defile and destroy nature was considered akin to doing the same to the Creator and disrespectful to God, to wit. Hence, unlike in present times, forests were never clear-cut to make way for agriculture and areas were never ripped up or desecrated beyond recognition when mining for the extraction of metals, minerals, and gemstones. This vision kindled very old memories in James' mind!

James could see, from the perspective of memories of this incarnation in Ananda, his compatriots were so highly evolved as to be beyond anything that we could comprehend in the present time span. They knew inherently, that killing trees was killing themselves... and also killing the highest expression of God in Ananda. Additionally, the people emulated the example of the trees, plants and animals and never used or possessed more than they needed for their immediate needs. And because the people knew all their needs would be met, they never entertained shortages of resources or land; there was no evidence of the pernicious effects of greed and hoarding. So a state of Zeitgeist, an equal sharing of resources depicted in the 2011 movie, *Thrive*, was essentially the Earth operating system in Ananda.

The people were from civilizations and cultures that had a far longer timeline than anything that ever existed here. Therefore, they had experiences beyond anything today's inhabitants of Earth have ever had. Thus, they had already made their mistakes, if any, in a time span which would be hard for us to perceive. But for these civilizations, because of a long history of respecting all God's creations, a pervasive field of shared thoughts and ideals existed. These viewpoints became the normal operating system for an entire civilization and was promoted by the longevity/extended life spans of the populace, which could be up to a thousand years and even beyond!

Additionally, since these people came from civilizations that operated in the fourth and fifth dimensions, they also had the ability to conceive of more and perform more than is possible in the third dimension operating system that has been prevalent on Earth in the last few thousand years. The benefit of these higher dimensional operating systems cannot be under-estimated. And yet James sensed Earth would be moving into these more prolific fourth and fifth dimensional energies and would in fact unleash a "Golden Age" on Earth.

Although there was a religion similar to Hinduism and the science of Yoga in Ananda, which involved the science of the union of God and man, the most important actions that were performed by people on a daily basis were actually extended sessions of meditation that lasted an hour or more. Additionally, people performed sacred prayers, called Sanskrit mantras, which was just as important as were the mediation sessions. These mantras were performed consecutively, at least 108, just as is completed using Catholic rosaries.

These concepts really resonated with James as he had been practicing the special meditations, specifically Pranayam from Kriya Kundalini Yoga and also recited many Sanskrit mantras daily. Unlike a rosary, which is performed in Latin or English, these mantras are performed in Sanskrit, which even today is considered a sacred language. A rich, poetic language, it contains vibrational power/cymatic properties capable of eliciting emotional and physical healing and bringing humans and other forms and objects into alignment with the existing Divine templates of perfection.

James knew putting sand on a table, with a speaker underneath it and then playing or reciting a Sanskrit mantra could document the vibrational power. What happens on the tabletop is the formation of geometric forms, especially the *Shree Yantra*, which is considered an auspicious, sacred symbol in Hinduism, which involves certain "sacred geometries."

These templates/geometric forms, James knew from previous knowledge, are clearly visible on the atomic level of creation! These cymatic (vibrational) properties likewise affect the binary pair's computer codes that comprise DNA and make it possible to alter and repair… although this was rarely, if ever, necessary in early Ananda. James also acknowledged that stimulating the telomerase strands at the end of the DNA through vibrations would reprogram the DNA and extend human life spans!

And the two most powerful of these prayers/mantras, *The Gayatri* and The *Maha* Mrityunjaya, came to be known as the most potent and auspicious of all mantras. James had an affinity for these mantras and practiced each of them daily. Both of them honored and praised the majesty and power of the Sun. And the people of Ananda knew, at the most fundamental level, that the Sun was an imperative component that fostered the existence of Prana/Chi/life force, which are the properties of God. This significantly increased the vitality of nature and the people themselves! For James, this Sun worship was simple yet profound, for without Sun there was little chance for life to exist, or at least as we know it here on Earth or even in other solar systems and galaxies!

These varied practices, including meditation/Pranayam and Sanskrit mantras, had a twofold effect, which was highly beneficial for the practitioners' thereof, as James was well aware. The meditation brought vastly more quantities of light energy into the body, similar to the Sanskrit mantras. This light was called Prana; comprised of photons, it occurred when a special meditation, *Kriya Kundalini Pranayam*, was performed. The meditation caused the light factor in the body to be enhanced and compounded exponentially. It could be augmented even more by mentally focusing more hydrogen into the body, which then caused an alchemical manifestation of higher combustions… resulting in more pranic energy and the resulting electrical field commensurate with it.

The Sanskrit mantras bathed the body with the cymatic properties of sound and vibration, which was composed of phonons. These phonons and photons, as previously discussed, were/are components of atoms. They cause the frequency and vibrational rate of the body to be lifted to a state of Divine Consciousness and a state of bliss or great happiness. The same results of higher consciousness also came from practicing the Pranayam breathing meditation, likewise.

So as a result of these two practices, the bodies of thee people of the Indian Civilization known as Ananda were more like light and less like dense matter than other people. This was most revealing for James, as it was in fact his goal to manifest a body of light, as opposed to a body of so-called dense matter. For the people of Ananda, the practice resulted in the ability to live in a state of radiant health and have no need for doctors; none existed, nor did any hospitals. These "light type" bodies were basically unaffected by injuries— wounds or bone breaks. And yet, even though the bodies were very close to a state of perfection, the people still performed daily stretching exercises, which were called Yoga Asanas.

James had pre-existing knowledge of all these things and the ability to perform them, yet it was exceedingly interesting for him to see how they were accomplished during this very early period on Ananda/Earth. This stretching—the Yoga Asanas—keeps light/prana flowing more vigorously and completely through the body. The early people of Ananda realized millions (billions) of years earlier, their bodies did not function as well as when they daily stretched and exercised. Also, they knew these stretching exercises kept their brains functioning better, akin to finely programmed computers that do not necessarily have to degenerate and malfunction, but can to continue to thrive and function at a very high level of performance on all levels, regardless of old age!

Additionally, the people realized that they actually needed very little food to live healthful and radiant lives and the food they did eat was concentrated on the types of food that were alkalizing to the body. Basically, the people were vegetarians and pescarians (fish eaters), which means they did not eat flesh, except those pescatarians who did. This new understanding was quite interesting to James, as he too was naturally drawn to the vegetarian and pescatarian diets as he progressed in his spiritual knowledge of things.

Also, none of the Anandan's food was processed and thus was consumed in its natural state. Because of their diet, and Anandan's body was always in an alkalized state, which further promoted their health because they did not imbibe alcoholic beverages or consume much food which contained sugar, except in the natural state of fruits. And the sugars they did consume were low or no glycemic, similar to products of which we are currently aware, like: *Stevia* (used for more than 1,500 years by the Guaraní peoples of South America, but only becoming popular in the U.S. in the 1980's), *Xylitol* (a product discovered by German and French chemists in the 19th century), and *Erithrol* (a product discovered in 1848 by British chemist, John Stenhouse), as well as black strap molasses and maple syrup.

In an alkalized state, the people of Ananda were in perfect health because no foreign organisms could live in their bodies. Additionally, in a condition of alkalinity, more prana/electromagnetic force could enter their bodies, similar to how an alkaline battery has more energy than a nickel-cadmium battery. Some of them were even Breatharians, who did not eat food and only drank water. The more of the "light factors" that existed in the bodies of these people, the easier it was to be a Breatharian. The people, who engaged in prodigious amounts of Pranayam and the recitation of many Sanskrit mantras, were the same ones who could actually transition into the Breatharian mode of living!

James was astonished to see just how far back in history these philosophies went, because he and Dr. Robert Newton had discussed how to achieve a Breatharian lifestyle in Chapter Eleven of A *Map to Healing and Your Essential Divinity Through Theta Consciousness*. Additionally, Dr. Newton had interviewed film director P. A. Straubinger, following his production of the documentary, *In the Beginning There Was Light*. Straubinger engaged his host in a lively discussion of the Breatharian lifestyle on the *Real Conspiracies with Solutions* radio show

Basically beyond comprehension for most people today, these Breatharians fervently believed their bodies could be nourished better with pranic force, which they breathed into their bodies during Kriya Kundalini Pranayam. This pranic force is comprised of electromagnetic energy, omnipresent throughout the entire Cosmos. Likewise, the human body is enveloped in a field of electromagnetic energy so there is a pre-existing sympathetic resonance between them. This early populace knew this energy definitely emanated from the Creator and was the ultimate source of nutrition!

They also understood that eating and digesting food consumes more Prana/life force than the energy released from it! People were also fully aware that if a person's emotions were not balanced and serene that it could well lead to overeating to compensate for feeling emotionally stressed. Additionally, they recognized that emotional factors cause sickness, disease and accidents, and avoided them through controlling negative emotions through practicing Pranayam and the recitation of Sanskrit mantras.

As James could clearly see, these people regularly lived to a thousand year lifespan and more. Again, this was due to the Pranayam meditation and Sanskrit mantra they performed daily. Of these concepts, James had personal knowledge through his daily practice of these protocols. Some people, through advanced yogic practices had transcended death and existed as immortals. There were protocols for this level of existence in Kriya Kundalini Yoga. The transcendence was achieved by entering a state of Samadhi, which is manifested through the Pranayam breathing meditation and the recitation of Sanskrit mantras.

In Samadhi, the body enters a state of breathlessness and the heart stops beating. At first the state will occur for a short period of time, about twenty minutes, and then extend to an hour and increase incrementally. These practices were part of James' daily routine, but he had not yet entered the state of Soruba Samadhi!

After many years, and sometimes decades of devoted and disciplined practice, a person would finally enter Soruba Samadhi, where they would permanently cease to breathe or have heart functions and enter the state of immortality of the body. This was possible because the body was fully supported by Prana/life force/God force… in its perfectly intended state of original creation. Although not everyone wanted to achieve Soruba Samadhi, because of the dedicated practice and assiduous amount of work necessary to achieve it, everyone knew and believed it was a possible scenario.

Thus, it was not considered exceptional or beyond the ability of the populace at large at that time! In fact, the people who attained this divinely exalted state of being were known as Kriya Yoga Siddhas and were greatly revered among the population. James was able to telepathically communicate with these great teachers and masters, the Siddhas. What he craved was the discipline to enter and live continuously in the higher dimensions they inhabited. He knew he was close to achieving this when he was incarnated in Ananda but his life was ended before he succeeded in such!

Sexuality was not considered a taboo subject or practice and accepted as a natural way for a conjoined man and woman, to boost the Prana/life force/God force in their bodies and also create a portal to attain a temporary Samadhi experience. James was starting to sense the same sexual attitudes he had in this incarnation may well have come from his incarnation in Ananda.

James could see the concept of promiscuity did not really exist in Ananda. It was known that if a man and a woman had a long-term relationship, they could only be benefitted from an extended physical relationship. Additionally, sex was more considered a long, drawn out process as opposed to a very quick and intense coupling, where the focus was just on "fun with friction." This was codified in such books as the *Kama Sutra,* which was based on the concepts of Tantra.

In Tantra, the entire sexual process is an extended affair and the result is the building of increased sexual energy, which is an intense pranic force. When an orgasm between the partners is finally reached, it creates "mind shattering" amounts of energy that both partners frequently scream out loud, seemingly in a state of pain, but rather in a condition of unbelievable pleasure, ensconced in Divine energy!

The screaming is the result of the tremendous amounts of Prana/electricity/life force coursing through their bodies, which creates a state of extreme euphoria and long lasting bliss. James loved this intense state of sexual and spiritual bliss, which was created in the past and present with Ann. There is never boredom experienced by either partner and as such, no need to consider what sex would be like with another partner; it was already far more than could be truly perceived and completely appreciated with your current partner! James was thinking, *this really sums up Ann and myself... we are so blessed!*

James also saw a lifetime in early Ananda where he was with a woman who looked just like Ann, his current wife, except her skin and hair were darker and her nose was broader. But for James, it was unmistakably Ann. The kind of love they shared in this lifetime was replicated in early Ananda, but at an even more intense level. A lot of the intensity was the result of the lush naturescape surrounding them—the overall energy of the trees and plants and the amazingly deep love that pervaded the peoples of Ananda. The sexual liaisons between James and Ann were so intense at this time, the very though of them sent chills down James' spine.

Since there was an abundance of pranic energy created and shared during sex, a state of peace and tranquility pervaded the entire society. This intense field of prana created during sexual conjoining literally magnified the energies of God and there were never any thoughts of conflicts or wars. This peaceful existence also had to do with a balance of the masculine and feminine energies, where neither a patriarchy nor a matriarchy existed alone, but rather were blended!

Neither resources nor effort was ever wasted on wars; they were directed toward the improvement of society and creating very highly developed art expressions and a music infused society. There were also devotional temples where people gathered to praise God through meditation and the chanting of Sanskrit mantras. James could see he too was involved in artistic and musical expressions, which were also a part of his current life. *Interesting,* James thought, *how things bleed through to our later incarnations, via these things and my connection to Ann.*

But for James, the fact that the people of Ananda were very aware of myriad forms of nature, and noticed over and over again that triangular forms manifested themselves repeatedly throughout the various types of fruit, in fractal forms, was an amazing insight. The Anandan's somehow realized that if they replicated these triangular forms in the construction of buildings and bridges, their structures would be vastly stronger and capable of withstanding the force of earthquakes in the spans in bridges and large buildings and temples!

Although the Anandan's did not have pyramids, per se, their temples included spires that served much the same purpose for increasing tensile strength. These spires, through the apex, accumulated and amplified Pranaic energies and the electromagnetic force contained within the Prana. Inside the temples it was easy to attain the shift to a higher state of consciousness when performing the Pranayam breathing and the Sanskrit mantras. So with these things enhanced, perceived, and actually felt within the bodies and minds of the people inside of the temple, it was a catalytic experience—on a super highway to God consciousness and Samadhi. Everything occurred faster and easier! James could actually relate this to his own earlier life experiences inside the pyramids in Egypt.

Ananda was but the first of spiritually evolved societies and the exalted state experienced by her people was further promoted because resources were not hoarded or controlled by one person or family or organization. This meant that there was no need for governmental organization and the smothering/liberty robbing effects of such organizations! So this was the first manifestation of Zeitgeist (the equal sharing of resources) and exopolitics on Earth, a concept introduced by Dr. Alfred Webre, as a discipline of the study of law, governance and politics in the Universe.

The people of Ananda lived in a state of "selective choice" wherein there were very few rules and regulations, if any at all. James felt his experience of the basic way of life in Ananda might well be fueling his interest in The Thrive movement, where individuals seek to reach peak physical and mental levels, and the Zeitgeist concepts of the sharing of all things.

Eventually, this exalted society would descend below its magnificence, ascend again; as time passed through four different time cycles of more than 200,000 years, the four Yugas totaling 4,320,00 years. The sequence was repeated several times until it reached the lower stature of today! As previously noted, the various time cycles and levels of evolvement commensurate with each one were called Yugas, which delineated recurring cosmic cycles of enlightenment or a lack thereof. One thing for certain... when the English colonized India in the 1800's they lowered the religious ideals and adapted a country that once was a natural food exporter to one that is a food importer!

According the Sanskrit text translations to which James had been exposed, the world would go into a mini Sat Yuga, which would be an exalted state of being for humanity on Earth—a "Golden Age." This could not come too soon for James! *The sooner the better*, he thought, *considering how dysfunctional the world has become geo-politically, geo-economically, environmentally and theologically!*

Also, it appeared as revealed in *The Ramayana* and in *The Bhagavad Gita*, there were two different nuclear wars in Ananda, the first over 300,000 years ago and the other about 5,300 years ago. These two different wars were fought against the forces of evil/darkness and also involved highly advanced aircraft and spacecraft, nuclear weapons and particle beam weapons. This truly indicates that the Anandan culture fell from its lofty perch within the direct influence of the Creator in complete peace and bliss and degenerated into conflict... where things reached a state of imbalance, not so much by the advanced technology, but how it was utilized in warfare.

James saw this was a recurring theme throughout most of the Earth's civilizations, as he engaged in many more sessions of remote viewing. This degeneration into war and conflicts in later Ananda would unfortunately create a morphogenic field of energy that would ultimately affect all succeeding civilizations on Gaia/Earth! This morphogenic field of energy was unseen, but certainly not something unfelt or without influence and effect on Earth!

When in his state of remote viewing, James also saw the Anandan civilization expanded in all directions, and powerfully influenced virtually all succeeding civilizations, in small and large ways. Even today in Mexico and Peru, there are religious ceremonies once a year that are based on Vedic/Anandan/Indian traditions. In these areas there currently exists ancient yantras, which are depictions of geometric forms, and still considered as sacred designations in India.

Also, Satguru/Siddha/Avatar Boganathur, of the Kriya Kundalini Yoga lineage, went to China around 10,000 B.C. and took a huge amount of spiritual knowledge with him to share with the people there. James could see that Boganathur modified his knowledge of Kriya Kundalini Yoga and created Taoism, a discipline that was openly accepted by the Chinese people. From Taoism came Tai Chi, a very relaxed form of marital arts that is still practiced today throughout the world, and the state sanctioned exercise there, to wit!

James could also see the pyramids in China, especially the Pyramid of Sensei, which is bigger than the Great Pyramid in Egypt. It appeared to James the pyramids were built by the Anunaki, an ET civilization that settled in Sumer, and encompassed both Iraq and Iran. James also saw huge pyramids in Bosnia and Serbia, which were discovered by archaeologists after he undertook his remote viewing sessions. They also seemed to be constructed by the Anunaki civilization!

| CHAPTER THREE

LEMURIA AND THE PEOPLE OF PEACE AND LOVE AND THE SUMERIANS WHO WERE MORE FOCUSED ON TECHNOLOGY

As James entered another session of remote viewing, he focused his intent and consciousness on the area of the Hawaiian Islands and other areas of Polynesia, which at one time were connected as one contiguous landmass. Here, another highly evolved people came to Earth about 250,000 to 350,000 years ago. The land was partially located in the area of the Hawaiian Islands, at a time when there was a large landmass as opposed to the smaller islands that now exist! It was called Lemuria and also Mu. Even today, the peace and love that emanate from these people is strongly discernible in the Hawaiian Islands and especially on the Islands of Maui, Hawaii, and in Tahiti. Nature still grows unbridled on many parts of Maui and the other adjacent islands—at least where modern civilization has not encroached.

The Lemurian's came from a highly spiritually evolved planet in the Pleiades and also from Ananda/India. In Lemuria, religion was not highly institutionalized. Since there were not innumerable rules about what a person could or could not do, it is understandable how the people developed such incredible psychic abilities and spiritual insights. Life was not wrapped up in religious dogma, nor squelched by a lot of repressive and irrelevant rules or controlled by a highly structured government. The control was unnecessary since people primarily operated out of their hearts and thus, were extremely peaceful and devoid of greed and envy. As James viewed this culture, he though just how much it reminded him of the Libertarian principle of government.

What James saw was far more preferable than the repressive socialism that infests most governments today. As in Ananda/India, people only consumed and possessed things for their immediate needs. In any culture, at any time in a world's existence, when people know all their needs will be met, it obviates the need to hoard resources!

Additionally, James saw that when everyone was highly telepathic, no one could easily fool or cheat another person; their thoughts would always belie and betray the words when communicated to their fellow humans! James thought, *how how much better society could exist if deceit was removed from the process of human conversations and have a consciousness centered in the heart chakra (heart energy and the love that flowed there from).*

He could see that much of the peace and love exhibited by the Lemurian people was the result of their strong immersion in nature, just as he had viewed in Ananda/India. On their own planet, in the Pleiades, inhabitants lived on a planet that was highly ensconced in nature because unbridled and rampant development of the planet did not exist. The people were prescient enough to realize that the diminishing of nature was the harmful to them. And that to honor and immerse themselves in trees and plants and flowers would enhance their peace and connection to their Creator! James continued to ponder when the controlling ruling forces on Earth, known as the Illuminati or New World Order would ever understand this concept and allow it to be manifested on

Earth, instead of playing a part in the deliberate intense exploitation of resources and people.

Anyway, this profuse immersion in nature was something the Lemurian's found in this particular spot on Gaia, which was so similar to their distant homeland. As soon as fruits or vegetables and were harvested from plants, vines and trees, they were almost immediately regenerated or re-manifested. Such profusion of food stocks made life very easy, leaving the balance of time to devote to art, literature, music, and chanting. The abundance of time available for these creative activities: dancing, painting and sculpture allowed for these important accomplishments. as there was an abundance of time to devote to such pursuits.

Such a state of agricultural bounty still exists in some semblance even today on Maui and other Hawaiian Islands, Tahiti, and the rest of Polynesia, which makes life vastly easier to live. The result of this cultural norm was an overall extremely happy and contented civilization where heightened levels of creativity are prolifically expressed and everyone feels an interconnectedness with each other; a non-duality. James could see this replicated how things functioned in the plant and animal kingdoms… in a manner of speaking. Likewise, he saw the strong connection, and how the people had developed an affinity for the ocean and its many fish and mammals. So strong were the telepathic abilities of these people, they could summon dolphins just through using their thoughts as a means of communication.

Similarly, the dolphins communicated with the populace and shared insights and spiritual wisdom with them! Since they did not have dolphins on their home planet, the

Lemurians were happy to receive the evolutionary spiritual visions, which the dolphins shared with them. The visions involved taking the mind to a deeper level of meditation through theta and delta brain/consciousness techniques, such as the Kriya Kundalini Pranayam meditation, practiced in Ananda/India.

James saw himself in a life in Lemuria where he was fishing in the ocean; where he made sure that neither Dolphins nor Sea Turtles were caught or injured in his fishing nets. The Dolphins appreciated this protection so much they would lead James and other fishermen to the areas where there was a higher concentration of fish stock.

The proliferation of love and inter-connectedness James witnessed between these and all other species touched him. He did realize, however, that the dolphins could have easily chosen not to share their knowledge of areas where the fish were more abundant! James fully understood this kind of sharing could very quickly change things on our current Earth and move us into the concepts of Zeitgeist… the sharing of resources and other things!

Much like the Anandans/Indians, the Lemurians were vegetarians and/or pescatarians, meaning that they ate mostly fruits and vegetables, and a few also ate fish. Other than fruits, their diet was alkalized, not acidified by red meats, or poultry and alcohol and highly sugared foods. Since their diet was alkalized, their bodies had alkaline pH balances, which allowed them to be inherently healthy and devoid of arthritis and related afflictions. They also enjoyed being sans heart and cholesterol issues, likewise, and were not susceptible to cancer, which is of epidemic proportions today due to a culturally accepted acidic diet. Likewise, an alkalized body state allows higher amounts of Prana to flow into and through the body, which not only contributes to a higher state of health, but also to a consciousness fixed on higher levels cognition and creativity.

James could see that the higher spiritual energy that literally surrounded Lemuria, as well the highly developed musical and artistic pursuits of the people, created a condition of true bliss for the people who dwelled there. Additionally, the energy and creativity was even more pronounced in the romantic relationships between the men and women of Lemuria. Their spirituality, together with music and artistic expressions, created a strong energy presence of God, which relaxed the people; in this relaxed state they felt the presence of God pretty much all the time!

Once again, James was able to tie into a lifetime in Lemuria where he was with Ann once again. As in Ananda, Ann had darker skin, but as equally a beautiful face and an intriguing and inviting presence. James and Ann would often take a stroll through the jungles of Lemuria. When they would get back from their jungle journey, they would go into their bedroom and lie down on their bed and caress and kiss each other with a deep connection. The longer they engaged in these amorous moments, which were usually over a very long time, the more the Prana/life force/energies of God would infuse their bodies and the lighter their bodies would become, both weight wise and in the sense of illumination.

When the couple finally moved in a more intense phase of the sexual process, the energy of their bodies sexually connected was so intense that both Ann and James would literally transcend into the fourth and even fifth dimension. In these levels, the sexual energies, which were simply the energies of God, would put them into an altered and higher state of consciousness that would last for hours. James could also see that he and Ann were not experiencing anything not experienced by many other Lemurian couples. This deep state of peace and tranquility pervaded all of Lemuria!

Because the Lemurians lived in an earthquake prone area, they acquired the knowledge and experience to build structures in a modular fashion, which allowed the buildings to withstand the intense shaking, swaying and thrusting associated with nature's phenomena. Relying on renewable or green resources for housing, smaller residential structures were constructed of palm and fern fronds and other branches and bark. Yet they used megalithic stones of lava to build their temples, where something akin to the Huna Pantheistic practices of Polynesia of today, occurred. This meant that Nature and the "spirits" related to it were worshiped and were the guiding force of the populace!

James saw that eventually most of Lemuria sank into the ocean, except for the scattered islands of Hawaii. James viewed the real chaos the Earthquakes produced in the populace as they occurred. This destruction had to do with plate tectonics, which are ever-present factors in this part of the world, and activated by volcanoes and earthquakes. Only scattered islands remained in place of a large continent. So some of these people returned to their home planet, but many others spread out and migrated to Atlantis, Egypt, Peru, Central America, and took their knowledge to transplant into new civilizations! But there was a remnant... a small band of people who remained in Lemuria, despite the disruptive conditions therein.

You would recognize them as the beloved Polynesians who intermarried with people from Tahiti, and to which Lemuria extended as an unbroken continent. Today, in Hawaii, remnants of the Lemurian people practice Huna religious traditions, which are Pantheistic in nature and actually revolve exclusively around Nature! Much the same exists in Tahiti, today as well. From his awareness James saw something that indicated the Tahitian people were not necessarily the progenitors of the Hawaiian's/Lemurian's as is viewed by the archaeologists of today.

The Sumerians, who were Anunaki from the planet Nibiru, were a race with mixed consciousness but more inclined to technology and building as opposed to spirituality and peace. Sumer occupied the area of Tigris and Euphrates Rivers and also occupied both Iraq and Iran. They inhabited Earth sometime between 350,000 and 450,000 years ago and it seemed as though there was always some kind of conflict, disagreements and war occurring between varying factions of Anunaki. These conflicts are detailed in the Old Testament, much of which came from records kept by the Anunaki!

Despite the fact the Anunaki appeared to battle a lot, and even detonated nuclear weapons, of which there are traces of even to this day via nuclear signatures, James could see the civilization also gave us some spiritual works including the Torah/Old Testament, which chronicled much of the history of the Anunaki. Inside Exodus in Chapter 14, verses 19-21 of the *Torah*, were the '72 Names of God' he previously studied and knew to be extremely powerful. Although the origins of these names is in question, most likely they were from Enki and Thoth.

The Anunaki also not only shipped gold mined on Earth back to their planet, Nibiru, but also consumed gold in the monatomic form. Although there are trace amounts of monatomic gold in our atmosphere, the Anunaki infused the essence of gold into water and other liquid forms. The benefit of this, as was previously mentioned, is that monatomic gold lengthens the telomerase strands at the end of DNA and thus works as a life extension protocol.

Most likely these regenerating properties of gold were the result of the complex octahedron form on the atomic level, which was made with the assumption it would release higher amounts of Prana/life force. It appeared to James the Anunaki/Sumerians never learned the advanced meditation techniques of Kriya Pranayam and Samadhi to lengthen the DNA telomerase strands, as did the Anandan's/Indians. They chose instead to use the monatomic form of gold to gain the desired effect; today this monatomic gold is sold as Ormus!

One thing became clear to James: although there was not a widespread spirituality practiced or even a reverence and respect for Earth by the Anunaki, the previously mentioned Thoth and Enki were actually the spiritual pillars of Sumer. James was of the understanding *The 72 Names of God* came originally from the *Torah,* but after his remote viewing of Sumer, he acknowledged the source of these principles could be traced back to the Anunaki and created by Thoth!

The Anunaki were builders of temples and pyramids and most likely constructed temples in Israel around Jerusalem and Syria at Baalbak, among other places. James could see where some pyramids were used to generate electricity via the technology used by Nikola Tesla at Wardenclyffe Tower in early 1900's New York, as an early wireless transmission station. The electricity was pulled from the atmosphere, and subsequently amplified into more concentrated electricity that required no outside energy. So the electricity was generated and distributed without wires and required no outside fuel or source of running water to generate energy, but used water to transport the electricity.

The Anunaki also interbred with the existing humans who were of inferior intelligence, but whose women were very beautiful... a trait still exhibited by Iranian women to this day. This interbreeding led to a mixing of Anunaki and human DNA. There are people who say genetic markers of Anunaki origin remain today, and much like the manipulation attempted today, that the Anunaki genetically directed during their time on earth. James also viewed having yet another lifetime with Ann in Sumeria; however this time James was the woman and Ann was the male counterpart. What an interesting twist this was for James; in fact he assumed the form of a beautiful Sumerian/Iranian woman and Ann was his husband, with a slightly large nose.

Again, the chemistry between these serial mates in various incarnations was powerful and created a state of bliss and compatibility between them that made their relationship a joyous union. James and Ann, in their reversed roles, were fluent in using "The 72 Names of God," which was another contributing factor that made their relationship meld into a very strong union.

Whatever the source of these names was, James knew the power of them as he had in this incarnation studied and repeated them for several years. The vibrational/cymatic power and effect these particular Hebrew words had on people and things was akin to something magical; similar in effect to the Sanskrit mantras James often repeated during meditation and other times throughout the day!

It appeared to James the Anunaki spent periods of time in Sumer when their planet was close to Earth and then depart before the elliptical orbit of their planet started to leave Earth's vicinity, repeatedly continuing the cycle. Some people today believe the Anunaki will return again, since they retain a vested interest in our planet. This should not seem so farfetched; other people believe the Anunaki created a firm control over this planet, and continue to rule it by proxy through the Zionists, Jesuits and Illuminati, when they cannot be physically present.

Certainly, this is a possibility, considering there is an entrenched power structure on Earth that rules things, superseding even the most powerful governments. The power of these groups is evident today, even as they commit numerous criminal acts involving banking and the instigation of wars and of the monopolization of Earth's resources, yet are never indicted or convicted of their gross criminal acts.

From the beginning, the Anunaki were obsessed with controlling the resources and people on this planet rather than being a benign and beneficial presence. This was the result of Enlil, the leader who ruled with an "iron fist." On the other hand, Enlil's brother, Enki, along with Thoth, loved the humans. But James had the strangest feeling Enlil was still running things on planet Earth. Enlil never shied away from a war and the fact that we have had a continual stream of wars on Earth provided James validation for these feelings!

| CHAPTER FOUR

ATLANTIS RISING—ATLANTIS SINKING

When the Lemurians translocated to the area of Atlantis, a region that covered much of what is now the Atlantic Ocean, there were myriad challenges in the transition. There was also a significant presence of Anunaki/Sumerians on Atlantis, not to mention the stark differences between their old and new locations, for both the Lemurians and Anunaki/Sumerians.

For one thing, although the growing environment for agricultural use allowed for the adequate production of food so the people could survive as a civilization, the food stocks produced were not nearly as prolific as in Lemuria. Fruit and vegetables could not almost immediately be replenished, since they were in a more temperate climate as opposed to the jungle ecosystem on Lemuria. For the Sumerians, this was a better growing environment than a hot desert, but the Lemurians found the sun was not as hot or tropical, which resulted in lower levels of Prana being directed to Earth. This was the beginning of the next remote viewing session undertaken by James, where he looked at the solutions to the problems the Atlanteans encountered.

The changes led the people to use science to improve agricultural harvests. At first, it was done in conjunction with nature/natural processes, which we call organic agriculture, today. The Atlantean scientists and farmers learned how to use humic shale, mycorrhizae fungus, animal manures, fish fertilizer, seaweed and kelp fertilizers, mineral supplements, gibberellic acid, hydrogen peroxide, ozone and mulching to increase their harvests and the nutrient density and bounty of their food supply. So the natural methods of growing, within the existing templates of nature, readily yielded tremendous harvests, comparable to Lemuria.

Again these were things James was versed in and familiar with and he knew the techniques would create high yields of fruits and vegetables and grains. The Atlanteans developed hydroponic growing systems, whereby vegetables and fruits were grown without soil and in water infused with plant nutrients. They then fine tuned this process and cultured fish in tanks below the hydroponic vegetables and fruits. They circulated water from the fish tanks, which was obviously laden with fish waste/manure, and dispersed it into the food stocks above. The method created much less need for added nutrients in the hydroponic system. This approach of growing food was called aqua culture and is seeing a re-genesis on Earth today. As James looked at all of this he wondered, *why did humanity ever discontinue employing these advanced means of growing foodstuffs?*

Even beyond agriculture, for various reasons everything on Atlantis involved more effort than on Lemuria. Since the forestation of Atlantis was considerably less than Lemuria, the Atlanteans looked for other building materials than timber, lumber, bamboo, banana leaves and palm fronds they had used on Lemuria. Their construction involved metallurgy to create metal structure skeletons to build houses and other buildings, and concrete based products to create floors and make blocks that were fitted together and made stronger with reinforced steel. Large, megalithic stones were also used in bigger structures. Lumber structures, culled from timber, were also used as a cheaper alternative to concrete and steel. But they were usually eschewed in favor of the more durable steel and concrete.

On Atlantis the "zero-point" technologies, akin to Tesla generating technology, were widely employed to generate large amounts of available electricity; the people used many different appliances that used this electricity. Alternatively, Lemurians did not frequently use appliances, and they relied on lighting inside homes and restaurants only for nighttime illumination. Lemurian lighting energy was provided by solar technology and stored by battery technology. Atlanteans also used geothermal magmatic power generation, whereby the heat from the Earth was used to create a portion of their electricity. They also used magnetic levitation technologies to generate power and propel their vehicles.

What James saw happening in Atlantis occurred more frequently, as further attention was applied to developing technology, domestic appliances, and conveniences… people started drifting away from their strong connection to nature. And as this gradually occurred, meditation began to play a less prominent part in their lives. Along with the transition came a level of crime that became a problem unlike any previously known in Lemuria or Ananda/India. Increased crime stimulated need for a more prominent government, which subsequently led to a dwindling of freedom and independence of the general populace.

All these changes led to nature no longer being viewed with reverence or respect. As this transpired, it was no longer considered taboo to remove plant and trees so formalized cities could occur and expand. Likewise, as cities expanded, the growth led to the industrial and domestic pollution of waterways and land areas. The change in people's diets… shifting from vegetarian and pescatarian eating habits to a carnivorous diet based on a higher consumption of various red meats and poultry. James recognized this as the beginning of the descent into degenerated states of consciousness, also known as beta consciousness.

At this point, logic and scientific methods started to replace an entire cavitation's connection to intuition and creativity! So essentially, the people stopped operating from their hearts and utilized their heads. Nature is known to sooth a person and activates the heart therein, whereas a highly technically developed society operates from the head (intellect), and the functions of logic are far more influential. With a clear insight, from his personal experiences in these matters, James could see the dangers of becoming logic centered; it seems to always create a separation between man and God. In fact James thought, *I could relate this to our civilization on Earth at this time!*

Also, as the diet of the people degenerated, so did their health. In rather rapid fashion the need for doctors and hospitals became necessary, whereas previously there was no need for them. Furthermore, as the alkalized pH balanced diet vanished because of the increased consumption of meat products, combined with the consumption of many alcoholic beverages, chronic illnesses began to proliferate among the population. As this occurred, the life spans of people were no longer in the thousand-year-range as in Lemuria, Sumeria and Ananda/India.

The negative effects that befell the Atlantean society would have been circumvented if the people had remained in consonance with what they brought with them from Lemuria. But an even more disturbing occurrence was the scientific research and applications it outstripped the consciousness of the people, and ultimately impacted the ability to responsibly use and control their technology.

In fact, in comparison to the genetic experiments and cloning that occurs on Earth today, what transpired in Atlantis vastly exceeded anything that has occurred here so far, until very recently. Atlanteans saw scientists combine fish forms with human, as Mermaids and Mermen were created. Additionally, men and horses were combined, which resulted in Centaurs we recognize from mythology, which really is not mythological at all. Men were also combined with goats and horses as per Bacchus, and horses were combined with birds, resulting in Pegasus. Certainly, there were other rather bizarre combinations; so bizarre the groupings appeared to be limited only by the imaginations of the scientists.

In his remote visioning, James watched scientists create super soldiers of incredible strength and cunning, similar to certain U.S. government programs today, like the DARPA Project. If you are not aware of the Defense Advanced Research Projects Agency, you might want to know they are responsible for both some of the best technology, such as the Internet, and the absolute worst, as found in Agent Orange, that has been developed in the past 50 years. Actually, the Centaurs and Pegasus were employed as fierce warriors for potential combat. James wondered, *just how long will it be before the Centaurs and Pegasus appear on our present Earth?*

Additionally, James was privy to Atlantean proficiencies in time travel. His visions showed their use of a pyramid form surrounded by rings made of various metals… creating an orgone effect, in which dissimilar metals actually create a more intense field of energy than the energy from the metals individually. All of these components were energized with a very strong electrical field. This created time warps and time portals that made going into the past and the future very easy to accomplish! The clearest analogy to this was from the movie and TV series, *Stargate.*

James witnessed a situation where the temperatures in Atlantis increased significantly, which created consternation about whether civilization could even continue to live in the increasingly hot temperatures. To counteract the increased warming, Atlantean scientists conceived the idea to spray an aerosol combination of barium, aluminum, strontium 90, and iron oxide into the atmosphere.

The spraying process was achieved through the use of aircraft and drones. In fact, the campaign to spray the chemicals into the air did actually lower the temperature a few degrees. James understood the process presaged the same type of aerosol spraying that currently occurs on a worldwide basis! Today, these aerosols are manifested as chemical aerosols, akin to the contrails that are dispensed from jet aircraft, except they contain toxic chemicals and last much longer, as the chemtrails fan out and disperse themselves. James shuddered and shook his head in a "no" fashion as he saw the myriad parallels between what he viewed in his remote visions and identical spraying occurring on Earth right now.

This cooling effect came at a high price for the people of Atlantis since they were becoming sick with respiratory problems and their immune systems were compromised… being assaulted with toxic metals, which were hard to detoxify/remove from their bodies. So there was more sickness and disease to treat; more doctors and more hospitals. *This sure seems similar to today*, James thought as he remotely viewed the scenario in Atlantis.

Even more importantly, by cooling the atmosphere the consciousness of the people was being trapped in the third dimension, whereas before they were able to survive in the fourth dimension. James recognized this dimensional shift was the result of the atoms in the atomic field moving at a slower rate, because they were being cooled, and emitted a lower level of Prana/life force/God force into Earth's biosphere. What he now understood was the agenda to counteract global warming on Earth was orchestrated to keep the people's consciousness low so they do not even realize they are being controlled by governments, corporations and religions. This is exactly what James saw occurring on Atlantis!

There were other things related to these changes; originally the Atlanteans had previously used herbal and energy healing in the few instances of sickness and disease they had to treat but then companies started synthesizing the active ingredient from these herbs and then began patenting them and charging exorbitant prices for the plants delivered as medicines. This would not have been so negative if the medicines actually worked in a long-term fashion. But this was not the case; the medicines did not heal much of anything at the level of causation and often had significant side effects, which is known as iatrogenesis. The side effects were the result of removing the buffering compounds the Creator had instilled within the herbs. As James viewed the negative modifications, he realized the same thing was happening in many countries, including the USA! *Well,* thought James, *I see the pharmaceutical folly was just transported from one time to another.*

James hurt for the people of the world as his remote visions reflected the life spans of the people were shortened even more as they actually degenerated into a lower state of health from the synthesized pharmaceutical medicines and the toxins being sprayed on them via the aerosols from the skies, as previously mentioned. The sad fact remained… these disingenuously manufactured pharmaceutical medicines, now promoted through legislation as herbal medicines, were no longer allowed to be promoted as the treatment of any specific condition, unless or until they had undergone extensive testing, even though the historical effectiveness of these medicines was widely known.

The pharmaceutical medicines made their producers wealthy, while the health of the people became very poor, unless they used the herbal medicines, which were hard to procure unless the people created their own herbal tinctures, infusions, oils, poultices, and healthy teas. Additionally, the pharmaceutical industry had succeeded in having the herbal remedies banned from being sold, since there were not sufficient scientific studies showing the effectiveness of their usage. A ridiculous action: the studies of the pharmaceutical medicines were wrought with all kind of toxicity and the side effects there from! Again, James was confronted with the similarity between "then and now" as the FDA made herbal medicine much more difficult to obtain and refuse to allow the usage of these herbs to be listed on their containers!

Many of these scenarios would have been obviated if the Atlanteans had realized that the Sun was making the Earth hotter because of three factors: The first had to do with the angle of Earth's axis, which was in a continual state of movement and in certain positions more solar radiation was able to penetrate Gaia's atmosphere and make things hotter; the second factor regarding the warming had to do with solar plasma eruptions released from the Sun; and the third factor was as the Sun of Gaia began to transit through the Milky Way Galaxy, it encountered an area with dust from exploded stars that contained large amounts of hydrogen and helium. This dust made the Sun burn hotter because it had more hydrogen fuel and also made the Sun increase in mass. Actually the second factor of the solar eruptions was directly related to the third factor; increased hydrogen being available to the Sun.

And again, James was privy to the same parallels happening on Earth with global warming, as a result of a greenhouse gasses hoax, which is just another way to extract more taxes from people already over-taxed. Of course there were greenhouse gases but their effect was exaggerated, as is now experienced on Earth. It was obvious to James that the Atlantean scientists were not aware of these three warming factors. If they had this knowledge, they would not have needed to aerosolize the atmosphere with toxic metals, because the increased size and energy of the Sun was pushing Gaia consistently further away from the Sun. This was a natural remediation of which the scientists were unaware! No one, including the scientists, was even concerned about the long-term use of the toxic aerosol being sprayed into the atmosphere. Actually, there were head/senior scientists who knew the Sun did not have to be cooled down, but they were being paid through large monetary grants to remain silent about their knowledge.

This was possibly the beginning of myriad long-term negative consequences caused by a lack of investigation and a failure to consider the negative significance of short-term decisions and actions! The information was being withheld from the population at large, being classified as a top-secret program. The mysterious ailments the Atlantean people contracted from the toxic aerosols were a secret that could not be kept! The Atlantean toxic global warming remediation program presaged the significant decline in the civilization's health, leaving James once more with deep thoughts, *This is similar to what is occurring currently on Earth and none of the governments will fess up to what is happening!*

Scientists then started experimenting with ELF (extra low frequency electromagnetic pulses and scalar waves), which they used for a variety of purposes, sometimes in conjunction with atmospheric aerosol spraying. These actions subsequently led to changing weather patterns and violent super storms. Powerful earthquakes also affected tectonic plates. From his remote viewpoint, James recognized the ELF experiments were also being used to disseminate propaganda and brain washing programs for nothing short of population control!

Eventually, the "big one," a super quake, occurred and caused the continent to rupture and split, unleashing several volcanic eruptions. The tectonic plate, on which Atlantis was located, began to sub-duct/sink into the Ocean floor, so the Atlanteans were forced to relocate to Sumeria, Egypt and Central and South America.

None of the connectedness of these changes escaped James' scrutiny! At least in part, if not entirely, the devastating earthquake, volcanoes and sinking of the tectonic plate was caused by meddling in the affairs of nature through the scientific experiments and weather modification! What was quite fascinating to James was how this ELF program shared similarities with today's HARRP/ELF programs, which have been undertaken by the USA, Russia, Norway, India and China! For James, these similarities were hard to ignore; they were glaringly self-evident! The bigger question was whether a few misguided megalomaniacs would lead humanity to the precipice of extinction!

In Atlantis, James saw the Lemurians were more focused on spiritual and agricultural pursuits whereas the Sumerians concentrated on technology, building and scientific activities; he could see the upper hand in this society was possessed by the Anunaki/Sumerians and that was the nexus of the downfall of Atlantis—too much science and not enough spiritual or artistic pursuits, wherein balance in life occurs!

James surmised there were too many similarities between current Earth and ancient times to ignore and many things that are in need of restoration to Aleph Kaf Aleph (a perfect state)! But before James left the numerous major crises he observed in Atlantis… tragedies that reoccurred on Earth, James focused his consciousness to determine whether he would find another incarnation with Ann. What James would uncover would be illuminating and then some!

James could see that he and Ann were scientists involved with the geo engineering of the climate in Atlantis and they even wrote a book together detailing the consequences of the long-term use of toxic aerosols in the atmosphere and the blowing of holes in the ionosphere with ELF/scalar waves. Writing the book was easy, getting it published much more difficult and getting it into the hands of the populace was even more difficult. This was because the government had anti-terrorist laws, akin to *The Patriot Act* and the NDAA that gave the government power to censor information. James was not surprised to find that censorship is exactly what happened when they published the book, *The Dangers of Atmospheric Manipulation*.

Their book was censored and they were imprisoned as terrorists, under the anti-terrorist laws. The couple was never brought to trial, but rather detained indefinitely in prison, without one! *Interesting,* James pondered, *this is happening in the United States of America, today, such as The Patriot Act and the National Defense Authorization Act (NDAA), among others, under the guise of anti-terrorist laws to protect us! With this kind of help and protection,* James thought, *who needs enemies?*

| CHAPTER FIVE

A NEW CIVILIZATION BRINGING THINGS BACK INTO BALANCE, EGYPTIAN STYLE "DANCING AND ACTING LIKE AN EGYPTIAN"

In his next remote viewing session, James viewed what happened to the remnants of the civilization of Atlantis, which was remains of the civilization of Lemuria and the thriving Sumerian State—and what happened when these civilizations came to Egypt. These émigrés faced the most hostile food-producing environment they ever encountered over the ages, except the people of Sumeria. Other remnants of the people of Atlantis went to Central America and South America where they found an environment that was lush with trees and plants and very easy to grow food. This was 13,000 years ago.

Since the Nile River, ran the entire length of the country in Egypt, the newly emerging culture knew they could intensively farm the land for about a mile or two on each side of the river. So while the desert was very harsh, a narrow part of it could be tamed and be made prolifically productive! Basically, crops could be gown year round because of the temperate weather.

About 5,000 years later, monsoonal type rains saturated the area for well over a thousand years and much of what was previously desert began to support plant life, but agricultural enterprises did not utilize much of the wetter area away from the Nile for farming or cities! The Nile River was known by everyone to be the lifeblood of the country.

Egypt was a fusion civilization with people from Sirius in the Orion's Belt, as well as the Lemurians and Atlanteans from The Pleiades, and the Sumerians from Nibiru. On the surface, these two civilizations worked in harmony, but there was always a struggle for power over who would control the government. This ultimately resulted in behind the scenes power conflicts, which at times erupted into the public domain.

Through their Pharaohs, the Sirians controlled the monarchy most of the time. The Lemurians/Atlanteans controlled the priesthood and had a large influence over how the government was administered; they considered the esoteric/spiritual influences an integral part of the everyday life of the average Egyptian citizen and government officials. The Sumerians were in charge of building the pyramids and temples that amply covered Egypt!

From his remote viewpoint James could see there was this already entrenched power structure, some of which came from Atlantis, which meant that the people were not as connected to nature as at the beginning of the Atlantean civilization. It was natural then for his immediate thought to be: *The influences of Pantheism, Nature and Natural Law are less prevalent, as always happens as highly structured governments stray from these balancing forces. My experience is that this type of government always eventually fails as a stable nation-state!*

From their native lands, Lemurian/Atlantean/Sumerian cultures brought the technology and applications of pyramid structures with them. In Atlantis, large granite pyramids were used to attract and distribute energy, as was replicated in

Tesla's "zero point" energy device designed in the early nineteen hundreds, at the Wardenclyffe Tower, in the U.S.A.

In Egypt this was done likewise with the Great Pyramid on the Giza Plateau. The Pyramid was known attract fire and light, and manifested as electromagnetic energy. In Greek, the word "pyros" was equated with fire, the root word of "pyramid." Regardless, the pyramid was designed to collect and amplify energy from electromagnetic fields and possibly even the strong nuclear force, which are ever present in the atmosphere. The pyramid did not create anything per se. but attracted what already existed and then accumulated and amplified it.

The pyramid form had something to do with the sacred geometries contained in Pi (3.1417) and Phi (1.168), which were an integral engineering mathematical component in their construction. These were concepts James had already studied, so viewing functional models of things was most enlightening to him, especially since these actual models do not exist right now or are just re-emerging on a small scale.

In Egypt and Atlantis, there are water canals/tunnels. And in Egypt these tunnels are filled with water, which even today surround the pyramids in Giza. The water was used to transport electricity generated by the Great Pyramid, and essentially worked like the tower created by the genius inventor, Nikola Tesla, in the early 1900's in the USA at the Wardenclyffe Tower in Long Island, New York.

Contrary to the popular beliefs of today, the Egyptians possessed high technological sophistication. Additionally, the Egyptians, as well as the Atlanteans and Sumerians, knew how to cut huge blocks of granite with huge masonry saws...

the machining marks from this cutting remain visible in the stones today. Even more amazing than their ability to shape these stones with machining, which would be impossible with crude hand cutting tools as has been erroneously claimed, was the way the stones were fitted together.

In actuality, James saw how the huge granite blocks were laid and fit together without mortar and with joints so tight that they could not be penetrated with a knife. Even more incredible was the ability to easily move the multi-ton granite blocks that composed the pyramid structures. The granite blocks were bombarded with lasers so as to speed up the movement of atoms, making the blocks literally lighter and able to be levitated into place. Sonic accelerators/generators were also used for this and they also increased the rate at which the atoms in the granite moved and thus they were likewise, made lighter and more easily maneuvered through levitation of the stone blocks. A non-literal analogy to this is changing boiling water into steam: the steam can move with less effort than the water from whence it came.

From his viewpoint, James was positive the idea that stones were dragged into place through ramps, rollers and pulleys was something dreamed up by people of limited perspective, using their own knowledge and then trying to back engineer it to a time technologically superior to now. Also at issue in James' mind was the precision with which the pyramids were constructed, within the parameters of plus or minus one-inch measurements on the four sides, which would only be possible today with satellite global positioning. From this perspective James could easily infer the builders of these pyramids had spacecraft and were of extra terrestrial origin! In fact, many depictions of spacecraft in petroglyphs around the world make that a moot point, as evidence of these craft is found in myriad places

Long before Pythagoras supposedly discovered the Pi (3.141) formula, the Great Pyramids previously utilized it as a template of mathematical precision millennia. James was in awe that, as was stated before, from a distance of over a thousand yards the sides of the pyramids were equal to each other within a factor of plus or minus one-inch. Also, Phi (1.1617), known to us as The Golden Mean, was also replicated as a formula throughout the structure of the Great Pyramid.

Besides the electrical generating capacities—actually electrical attracting abilities—of the pyramid, the great structures also effected a strong altering of consciousness when people meditated inside of them. James had previously discovered pyramid shapes resonate at the frequency of eleven hertz; quartz crystal resonates at this frequency likewise. Probably not coincidentally, the Great Pyramid had a quartz triangular capstone at its apex/peak, actually a quadrahedron form, which would just synchronistically attract a higher field or amount of energy, Prana/life-force, God force/energy.

Additionally, James discovered the human body contains a large amount of silicon dioxide, a component of quartz. So while there has not been detected an 11-hertz frequency within the human body, there was likely a sub-frequency of some type therein and in that regard, a coherence and resonance between all of these things—basically being mutually tuned and synchronized.

Securing the preceding information caused James to then focus his attention on a frequency within the human brain that is 7.83 Hertz, a deep state of alpha altered consciousness and sometimes an upper level theta consciousness state. This is something that is attained during an extended, deep meditation, or something that could occur during singing and dancing for an extended period of time. The deeper, lower brain waves would be amplified, especially during a session of deep meditation inside of a pyramid, which the Lemurian's were very proficient at accomplishing hundreds of thousands of years previously. Also, the Anandans/Indians achieved this state at least a billion years before the Lemurian's. This 7.83-hertz frequency was also part of the Schuman resonance as the inherent frequency of the Earth.

What James also learned was that diatonic note, C# (C sharp) also was an Earth frequency. So he tried to find a direct relationship between C# and the Shuman Resonance. When he reduced C# to a sub-audible level, he detected an 8.15 hertz frequency, but that was still not an exact melding of these two fundamental Earth frequencies.

Anyway, the confluence of all of these things allowed an experienced meditation practitioner to enter such deep states of meditation where breathing and heart functions cease to occur, yet the person continued to live and experienced no brain damage or harm to internal bodily organs. This was exactly what the devoted practitioners of Kriya Kundalini Yoga were doing in Ananda/India, before the Lemurian or the Atlanteans or the Egyptians; it was called Samadhi. In Egypt, it was called "Lotus Consciousness," but each exercise basically would take the person to the same theta/divine consciousness. This concept of "Lotus Consciousness" was something James had never encountered in his extensive study of Egyptian esoteric practices!

Besides the massive pyramids that were dispersed throughout Egypt, the people also built huge temples from sandstone columns, trusses, roofs and walls. Having already been in Egypt previously, James was intimately familiar with the magnificence and the huge scale of these monuments. The sandstone columns were three to four feet in diameter and in sections three feet high, were stacked one atop each other. The height of the columns could be fifty to seventy-five feet and obliques where made from granite that at times extended seventy feet tall. They were nothing more than modified pyramids and were used as energy accumulators, and to distribute electricity to the populace, as per the Tesla technology previously discussed. These temples, as well as the pyramids, were scattered throughout Egypt.

But certainly, the temples were most prolific in Thebes (now Luxor) as were the pyramids in Giza. The Temple of Luxor was located in Thebes; a template, replication, or representation of the human body, complete with the chakra energy points existing in the body. There were likewise many aspects of sacred geometry existing in the temple structure, including Phi and Pi.

At the temple of Karnack, there were many grand temples contiguous with each other on over forty acres and a lake, which reflected images of the temples. Truly the energy emanating from the sandstone columns was easily detectable because it was so powerful, due to the quartz crystal in the sandstone. These temples were built over a span of thousands of years, by different rulers/Pharaohs.

Meditating inside the temples created significantly altered brainwaves that led to exalted states of consciousness. But this was more of an occurrence for the temple priests than the population at large, which spent large segments of their time devoted to agriculture, artistic pursuits and construction projects.

As the population expanded, it put a strain on the land to produce enough food to feed the people, but it was accomplished, using organic methods of farming that included no petrochemical fertilizers or synthetic insecticides. James had even had three organic farms himself, and after experiencing the petro-based fertilizer and petrochemical insecticide revolution in the U.S. he was well aware of the current movement to return to organic methods of farming… to shun the agri-business model of using unnatural substances to grow food stocks! This was a superior approach to agriculture, anyway, because of the long-term deleterious effects of petrochemical, manmade fertilizers and insecticides. Petrochemical fertilizers inevitably lead to high salinity in the soil, making crops difficult, if not impossible, to grow. In a related manner, the petrochemical insecticides are toxic with long residual pollution, which contaminate groundwater and rivers and lakes and oceans. In all of these things, James had extensive knowledge and experience; he could appreciate seeing this at a point of a genesis in both Egypt and Atlantis.

While there were no forests with emotionally soothing properties contained therein, the cities basically were close to the Nile River, and it was this water element that could be as good an emotional palliative as a forest or jungle of trees and plants. Basically, the negative ions emitted from the water crashing in the Nile River, were mood elevating and emotional palliatives for the people who were exposed to the negative ionic fields of energy/electricity. The negative ion effect was much more pronounced then, than now, because there was no Aswan Dam to control the flow of water; during the spring rush, or the higher flow of water that ensued. James was aware a lot of research has been completed in recent times, which showed the benefits of negative ions on physical and emotional health!

A major figure in Egypt was Thoth. A documented personage in Egypt, he had an influence beyond that of any other person and was a guiding presence in both Sumeria and Atlantis. Thoth was considered a Netter God, not the ultimate God, but a person possessed of great knowledge and understanding who had transcended the cycle of death. He had the ability to travel between planets without the use of a spacecraft, using only a merkabah, which was a self-created ball of light or a body of light. From the planet Sirius B, it is this origin from whence Thoth's advanced understanding emanated, beyond all other personages in Egypt or any other place on the Earth, for that matter!

Thoth, depicted as the bird, Ibis, honed his skills and knowledge in Atlantis and Sumeria and was a major guiding force there, before translocating to Egypt. He had ruling influence in ancient Egypt, before the reign of the pharaohs and he worked with and within the priesthood, dispensing esoteric knowledge he shared with other netter gods, depicted as animals or birds, including Sekhmet, Anubis, and Horus, among others.

Thoth's great knowledge of engineering and construction was likewise instrumental in many major building projects in Egypt, including temples in Thebes/Luxor and certainly, The Great Pyramid in Giza. When the Pharaonic ruling influence was established in the ruling class in Egypt, he worked more in the background, but still had more influence than anyone else in Egypt.

Thoth wrote *The Book of Thoth*, which was a template of spiritual knowledge that guided the priests and subsequently, the populace. It was written in the hieroglyphic symbolic language that Thoth had created and transcribed. There were cymatic/vibrational properties to these hieroglyphic words, which focused on all the vowel sounds. It was these vowel sounds that were responsible for the symbols affecting physical bodies and objects since vowels have more resonating properties than consonants! James was frustrated he could not find a Codex that would give the keys to pronunciation of the hieroglyphs, but consoled himself with the belief it existed somewhere and would eventually be found!

James relaxed in his remote viewing, to watch the priests use the power within the hieroglyphic symbols and sounds, similar to the power of the Sanskrit language contained in mantras… not only to shift their consciousness to the level of theta trance divinity, but to actually manifest objects from the ethers/atomic field. He experienced a certain level of sadness, however, as he watched Egypt begin a slow descent from the zenith of spiritual knowledge; the rulers and even the priests became more enmeshed in bureaucracy and less influenced by the high spiritual forces and understanding upon which Egypt was originally formulated under the guidance of Thoth!

James knew he was previously a priest in the Temple of Luxor in Thebes because when he was visiting this temple in 1984, he was spontaneously regressed into a past lifetime while walking into the temple. But what he did not know until this particular remote viewing session was that his wife, Ann, was the wife of a Pharaoh. Who that Pharaoh was James could not ascertain, but that Ann was leading a life of royalty was easy to discern! Ann was a supporter of the arts and Egyptian styles dance and even she, herself, would often dance like an Egyptian!

Eventually, Egypt became so pervaded by the corruption that accompanies large bureaucracy, both governmental and religious, that it was conquered by the Greeks… first by the great General, Alexander the Great, and then later by the Roman General, Marc Anthony. By this time, the great magnificence of Egypt faded beyond anything resembling its zenith! At once, it was painfully obvious to James that the further any civilization moved away from the influences of Natural Law and Nature, the sooner it would eventually collapse or degenerate into mediocrity! So the question still lingered in James' consciousness, *why does this happen repeatedly, throughout history?*

Then James had an insight that this rise and fall might have to do with the Yugas of India, which were long cycles of times, as was previously discussed, wherein there are times that are more exalted on Earth, cyclically, and other times where things are debased! The bigger question in James' mind then became, *Can the exalted cycles of time be extended beyond a limited period of time and in contravention to the concepts of Yin and Yang, or light and dark, and can mankind always live in a state of exaltation?* The answer to that, for James, was within the 7th Name of God from Exodus in the *Torah*, "Aleph Kaf Aleph," which translates as reestablishing/establishing perfection on Earth!

CHAPTER SIX

THOTH MOVES TO GREECE AND BECOMES HERMES

So as James entered his next remote viewing session, he viewed the civilization of Egypt as it crumbled and the culture of Greece ascended. Much of this change resulted from the knowledge the Greeks had attained from interaction with the Egyptians. Additionally, the Greeks were recipients of knowledge from an extra terrestrial civilization thought today to be mythical; yet actually existed. James pondered a few moments how he had studied this in ninth grade history in Miss Juhl's class and recalled he was absolutely convinced all she taught was fabricated and myth, as opposed to the reality he came to experience.

However, James learned the leader of these ET's, Zeus, actually existed as more than a fantasy. It appears the people from this stellar civilization were the actual guiding or ruling force in Greece, although this information is not apparent in most historical records. These extra terrestrials possibly came from Nibiru, as did Pythagoras, who was also in Egypt and instrumental in the building of the pyramids and temples there. Or did he come from a more distant origination?

Pythagoras actually referred to his extraterrestrial origin and he also discussed other personages who came from there also. Pythagoras had much mathematical knowledge and he was venerated for the supposed discovery of the geometric formula, Pi (3.1417), which was a crucial element in the survey and construction of what came to be monumental building projects. But as was mentioned previously, Pi was used in Egypt and more than likely in Atlantis as well.

Thoth moved his home base from Egypt to Greece and became known as Hermes Trismegistus, and guided the people there, as did Zeus. Both Hermes and Pythagoras held knowledge for building temples that was as indispensible to the Greek as it was to the Egyptian civilization. And their knowledge and spiritual and scientific insights were distilled into *The Emerald Tablets of Hermes Trismegistus* and "The Pythagorean Theorem."

Basically, Hermes' *Emerald Tablets* was a very concise but all-inclusive declaration that conveyed all levels of existence were inter-related in a fashion of basic non-duality. In other words, all creation is interconnected through the all-pervasive energy field of the Creator as a fundamental denominator, signifying a common inter-relatedness between all person and things. This existence extended from the atomic level to the galactic realms! It also meant that there was no material reality separate from a spiritual/energy reality, but rather that the spiritual/energy level was the basis of all creation, not deteriorating matter!

James understood this to mean that not only were people interconnected with each other, quite literally, but also the connection extended to the plant and animal kingdoms. And it also meant that the inter-relatedness extended to people, plants and animals… just as the cutting edge science in Quantum Mechanics currently shows us actually exists!

The Pythagorean Theorem was mostly used to measure the angle of a pyramid by measuring the two sides and was geometrically notated as a2+b2=c2. This was an indispensible component that was later used in engineering structures, but was first used in the construction of the Greek temples, although this is not self-evident, it is reinforced in the construction thereof.

It was within these parameters that all of life flourished in Greece, with the great philosophical insights of Plato, Sophocles and Aristotle, among other great philosophers and teachers. This insight extended to the healing arts/medicine and the knowledge of Asclepius and his protégé, Apollonius of Ti'tyus (Tyana).

From Asclepius, who seemed to be a descendant of Zeus and a woman citizen of Greece, great knowledge of herbal healing was collected and practiced, so much so that people came from all over Europe and Asia to be healed by the great Asclepius! However, notwithstanding his great knowledge in herbal healing, Asclepius had a great epiphany that there was an even more superior way of healing beyond the use of herbs. This epiphany was of lucid daydreaming and leading a patient into an alpha-theta level of consciousness, somewhat like a hypnotic state, but deep enough to lead the patient to divine insight so the patient could heal themselves, sans any medicines. This process was actually similar to the first line of *The 72 Names of God* from Exodus 14, verses 19-21 in the *Torah* and considered part of the Kabbalistic knowledge of Rabbi's.

James could see from his remote viewpoint he had worked with the great legend, Asclepius, learning herbal healing and then later the lucid daydreaming techniques that were intuited by this great leader. James thought it was interesting how these things from the past paralleled his present life as a healer. This was clear evidence of "bleed-throughs" from a past lifetime that affect us in our present incarnations.

His wife, Ann, on the other hand, worked as a liaison between the ET rulers and the Greek Kings. The ET's resided in their space craft on and above Mt Olympus, and while Ann was of Greek origin, she was favored by the ET's because of her fair skin, long hair, stunning beauty and great intelligence! Certainly there was also a sexual attraction; there are records in the so-called mythology of Greece of these ET's/Gods mating with the beautiful Greek women on many occasions!

Thoth-Hermes was also known as Enoch, in the Kabalistic tradition and "rested" on the upper rungs of the Tree of Life, as an angel just below Metatron, who was at the top of the tree along with Archangel Michael... who are below Yahweh at the top of the "Tree." This information is provided for the purpose of revealing just what an important and pervasive presence Thoth-Hermes-Enoch merited on Earth/Gaia.

Hippocrates was often considered the father of Western Medicine, even though he, too, only used herbal remedies. Asclepius predated Hippocrates and was the acknowledged father of medicine in Greece and even later in Rome. Medicine aside, the Greek civilization began to decline as corruption became rampant in the city-states of Greece, where much of their learning and engineering was transferred to Rome.

Rome thrived for a shorter period of time than Greece and was a highly militaristic culture, bent on conquering as much of the world as possible. Although the Spartans were fierce warriors, this was not the mind-set of the people of Greece. Regardless, neither Greece nor Rome experienced a lengthy Golden Age, as did Egypt, Atlantis, Lemuria and Ananda/India. James deeply felt the Golden Age of each succeeding civilization was shorter and, in his perception, the shorter term stemmed from the drifting away from the crucial Nature connection James believed is needed to keep things in balance and uncorrupted via Natural Law!

In both the Greek and Roman civilizations, the growing environment was somewhat harsh, being a dry type climate, commonly called the Mediterranean. Each of the cultures concentrated on growing olive and other fruit trees (especially figs), wheat and more drought tolerant vegetables, which could be augmented with sheep and fish. But since their diet contained the flesh of animals, the vitality, intelligence, and spiritual knowledge and practices of the people was no longer highly concentrated, even though the fruits, vegetables and herbs they consumed had a high nutrient and medicinal value.

Rome was one of the first documented examples of deficit spending; there was more than one emperor who decided to overspend the revenues available to the state treasury. James saw how this actually caused Rome to collapse and descend into widespread disorder and chaos. Certainly James also figured with a deficit spending of more than 80 years in duration, it was a matter of time until this transpired in the U.S.

While life in Greece represented a theme of Pantheism and a devotion to nature, it was nowhere close to what existed in the civilizations of Ananda/India and Lemuria, which were more lushly vegetated Without the intense energy field of nature, these civilizations could not replicate the magnificence of those peoples who preceded them! The theme in the declination of man as he deviated from the values of Nature was clearly evident to James, once again!

| CHAPTER SEVEN

ENOCH/HERMES, THE ISRAELITES AND YESHUA

As James entered his seventh remote viewing session, he intuited that he would follow Thoth/Hermes again, but to a different location. Indeed, he did follow Thoth/Hermes after he left Greece and went to teach the Israelites as Enoch, Israelites developed a deep spiritual system based on the mystic and esoteric knowledge of Enoch, who was also Hermes and Thoth. But much of their knowledge came from the information in the Sumerian Tablets, which were talked about in Zecharia Sitchins' books, including *When Time Began* and *The Twelve Planet*. This included the Ten Commandments and the Kabbalistic *The Tree of Life*. This system was known as the Kabbalah. *The Tree of Life* designated a hierarchical system of Angelic beings—entities that were within the strong influence of the Creator—as opposed to the wily-nily existence of the average human and the uninspired existence that was part of such a consciousness! Interacting with these angelic presences was believed to raise the consciousness of someone studying the belief it would bring them to a closer communion with God.

The language of the Israelites was Hebrew, a sacred language as per Sanskrit and the Egyptian hieroglyphs. The sacredness of this language emanated from the fact that its vibrations and sounds had cymatic properties—creational forces of sound and vibration that can physically affect people and objects. These things are affected by these phononic forces, which are a property of atoms. Hebrew most likely was strongly influenced by the Anunaki and Sumerian cultures developed on Earth much before the time of Israel.

The Kabbalah contained *The 72 Names of God*, which was the cymatic properties of the Hebrew language that made the names so powerful, in that they could completely change the outlook of a person from a lower/base consciousness into a divine perspective and even affect objects by modifying their atomic properties. Beyond this, myriad things could be materialized from the ethers through the proper intonation and application of these names of God. There are also healing properties to these names, as per the 5th Name of God, Mem Hey Shin (both means, and embodies, healing)!

These things allowed a highly spiritualized population to flourish, although there were not as many temples as found in India, Atlantis, Egypt, Greece and Rome but there were magnificent temples in Jerusalem, especially the Temple Mount. The Rabbi's were the priests of the temples.

Eventually, a young Rabbi, a Rabboni, would appear on the scene in Palestine/Israel as it was beginning to decline. His name was Yeshua, which we now know as Jesus. He arrived from a distant star system by travelling through a time portal/worm hole/energy vortex. James remembered how Yeshua arrived on Earth in this manner, having read of the events in *The Secrets of Sion*, by William Henry, Of course, this understanding is in complete contra-distinction to the birth and initial appearance of Jesus on Earth, yet it could well be more accurate than any other recollection of this matter!

After studying the Torah and the Kabbalah, Yeshua began preaching to the people and showing them how they were straying from their spiritual foundations. He caused great concern in the Rabbinical order through his teachings. Yet the Rabbi's really could not touch Yeshua because many thousands of people would come to hear him teach.

The throngs of people were not only transfixed by the simplicity and clarity of Yeshua's teachings, they were amazed by the humility he displayed, unlike the Rabbi's in the temples. Yeshua's fame was spread far and wide, throughout the land of Israel and surrounding areas like Jordan, Syria, and Egypt because of the miracles that he manifested in front of the people. Yeshua healed thousands of people; he even raised people from the state of death. He also manifested things from the ethers, like food, such as fish and bread.

What the people did not realize is that Yeshua had studied with Egyptian priests, Buddhist monks, Kriya Kundalini Yogi's and Vedic Hindu priests. This all occurred during the so-called "lost years of Jesus" noted in the *Bible*. It was the combination of these things, as well as the additional Kabbalistic knowledge that Yeshua had learned and could practically apply, that was responsible for his healings and manifestations. *The 72 Names of God* was also an integral part of this dynamic. It was these disciplines and teachings that infused so much prana/chi/life force/God force within Yeshua that his body was basically energy and not dense matter. This fact was often depicted in the paintings of Yeshua, which revealed a huge orb of light around his head and body.

So it was Yeshua living in this state of high energy and knowing that this was the true essence of all other humans, which allowed him to heal, raise people from the dead, and manifest objects such as a voluminous amount of food. Such names of God such as Hey Resh Chet (connected to the light) and Ayin Resh Yod (the certainty that God is always there for us) aided Jesus in performing his so-called miracles. Eventually, because of his ability to transcend time and space and the accepted limiting laws of society and religion, the Pharisee's, the protectors of the Judaic teachings and writings, conjured up an indictment of Yeshua and had the Roman occupier's prosecute him, for his perceived transgressions against the teachings they jealously guarded.

Yeshua not only had not committed any transgression against the laws of the Creator or Natural law, he actually fulfilled the highest aspects of these things in deference, respect, and submission to God. This was just the playing out of a recurring theme on Earth wherein authorities, envious of those with superior abilities, insights, and understanding of things, were brought down and punished for being "ahead of their time."

Jesus' so-called death was not in fact a death at all but rather a demonstration of Soruba Samadhi, an eternal state of deathlessness in a human body. Additionally, Jesus did not die for the sins of humanity but rather to show the populace the immortality of the body through Soruba Samadhi. The only sin ever really committed by any person of planet Earth is believing they are anything less than perfect, immortal and divine, as per Aleph Kaf Aleph (restoring things to their perfect state).

The Jesus scenario was something that would happen many more times. In Greece, Socrates drank hemlock rather than being tried in court and killed by the authorities. During the Dark Ages, Middle Ages, The Renaissance or even modern times on Earth, numerous other souls, beyond just Joan of Arc, were killed likewise for their unconventional ideas! Another one of these casualties was Babul, the founder of the Baha'i faith.

The following things that James saw really kind of freaked him out in regard to the deviousness involved, Unfortunately for the Israelites and humanity in general, the exaltedness of Israel would eventually a become state where a group of secular Jews, known as Zionists, would hijack Judaism and use the cover of its great teachings and distort and pervert them to enslave the entire modern world! The Zionists did such a good job of co-opting Judaism that few if any people would ever question the authenticity of their ideas or the morality of their actions. Today, there does not seem to be much concern that the Zionists, are in gross violation of the *Ten Commandments*, the "Golden Rule," *The 72 Names of God* from Exodus in the *Torah* and "Natural Law." Learning and seeing these things via remote viewing was very disconcerting for James, as in fact, he viewed multiple lifetimes where he was a Rabbi and retained very good feelings and memories related to these lifetimes!

One thing was very certain to James and that was when he revealed the diabolical and devious actions of the Zionists, there would be an outrage against him and he would be labeled anti-Semitic. As vociferous as such outrage would be, James found blind acceptance and vindication of the indefensible killing of innocent people, such as Palestinians at large… as ludicrous, no matter how they were justified, which was always through some type of propaganda, demonizing someone not in favor. Additionally, James could not really fathom how the Zionists made everyone feel guilty about the Nazi Holocaust of the Jews when they were de facto doing the same thing to the Palestinians, despite their protestations to the contrary!

It was also well within James' knowledge that there were few Semites even still alive, among the Jewish sects, so it would be impossible to be against something that did not exist. Beyond this, James had a deep reverence for *The 72 Names of God*, from Exodus in the *Torah* and exalted these teachings above all else in the *Torah* or the *Bible*. For him, everything else in the Old Testament could be discarded once someone had the knowledge and understanding of these powerful and insightful names.

James knew as a fact the Zionist controllers of Israel had little if any knowledge of *The 72 Names of God* and that if they practiced such teachings they could never justify killing and smearing the reputations of people who did not agree with them. James was tormented by the fact most Jewish people believed Zionism was a good thing, as they are taught the concept from birth. James also thought, *I do not want to be labeled anti Semitic or marginalized by the Jewish people because I love their '72 Names of God' and study and practice them, but it might be inevitable via the 'hive mentality'!* The problem here was that it is difficult for most people to learn new things and let go of their old knowledge and understanding of things, especially when they have been taught something from the time of their childhood!

Anyway, one other thing James viewed was the temple of Baalbek in Lebanon where huge, multi-ton stones were used in its construction. As magnificent as were the big stones used at the Temple Mount and other places in Jerusalem, they could not match the grandeur of the stone blocks used in Baalbek. Before his remote viewing session, James had no idea of this magnificent monument in Baalbek! Later he would view pictures of this temple in Zecharia Sitchin's, *The Earth Chronicles Expedition.*

Just as James was about to end his remote viewing session, information started flooding in to him regarding the New Testament. He could see the books collated into the New Testament were not written by the Apostles but rather by the Roman ruling class, as a means to control the populace at large... filling them with guilt, and thus being able to manipulate them very easily because they were convinced they were sinners. Interestingly enough, the Gnostic texts, from the Essenes, were not included in the New Testament but were written at the time of Jesus and not several centuries afterward like the New Testament books. Roman Piso chronicles this information in *Piso Christ*; the Gnostic texts are discussed in William Henry's book, *The Secrets of Sion.*

James thought he was done with his remote viewing session and then he saw Ann as a friend of Mary Magdalene. This was interesting since Ann and James often discussed how Mary Magdalene was not a prostitute at all and more akin to a disciple of Jesus and even possibly his wife or consort. Certainly, this was in contra-distinction to the denigration of women that pervaded the paternalistic Roman Catholic Church.

More than one psychic had already told James that he was in Jesus' inner circle. He could see this as a probability as he viewed many events that surrounded Jesus! Irrespective of the validity, it was clear to James that Christianity had been hijacked by the Roman ruling classes and then later the Roman Catholic Church. The word "Roman" preceding Catholic Church was extremely revealing as to the hijacking of Jesus' teachings and the intent thereof by people with an ulterior motive to control and enslave humanity! This was akin to what the Zionists did to Judaism and really perverted the beauty thereof!

James thought, *either of these scenarios would have been circumvented if the people were closely tied to and immersed in nature. There are few trees in this area except the Cedars of Lebanon.* James could clearly see this from his earlier remote viewing sessions!

James thought he was done with his forays into Israel and then in popped some more memories and pictures from a lifetime he spent with Moses, wandering through the desert. James had read things where Moses was in fact of Anunaki origin and considering he lived for more than 900 years, this would seem to be true since nine hundred to a thousand year life spans were common for the Anunaki. James could see that the "manna" that came from "the heavens" to feed the Israelites was actually descending from spacecraft, most likely of Anunaki origin. Although the people with James complained about having to eat manna every day, they would have perished without it and the water that was shared, likewise.

|CHAPTER EIGHT

GOING BACKWARD TO PICK UP THE TRADITIONS OF THE MAYAS

Moving backward in time, James went into his next remote viewing session. Retrogressing, in order to keep the lineage of Thoth/Hermes/Enoch intact, elements of the remnants of the civilization of Atlantis migrated to Central America as well as to Egypt, upon the sinking of Atlantis. There were some different major figures and presences for the Mayas known as Misol Ha, the god of the Sun. Yet, once again, Thoth appeared again in the form of Quetzalcoatl. The timeline for the Mayas has always been underestimated because all of the records in stone tablets and codex's have not been recovered, and goes back 13,000 years.

And it is this 13,000-year time period that coincides with that of Egypt where Thoth was likewise. James pondered, *so how could Thoth be in two places at once?* James found Thoth knew how to teleport himself through time and space and thus could easily transfer his presence easily, from one place on Earth to another. This thus would mean that his body was basically pure energy/spirit or at least largely comprised of these factors! He could move thousands of miles in a few seconds using worm holes/vortexes from one place to another, transporting himself with the use of major magnetic ley lines that crisscross planet Earth, in conjunction with vortexes/worm holes!

Since this civilization incarnated within the influences of Atlantis and extra terrestrial intervention that was present in

Atlantis and Egypt, it had highly developed systems of astronomy, science, arts and large construction projects, of which Quetzocoatl/Thoth was also involved. There were large pyramids and temples throughout Yucatan, Mexico and Guatemala. The stones used in these pyramids and temples were much smaller than those used in Egypt, due the fact that there were not stones of the dimensions as available in the granite and sandstone quarries in Egypt and Atlantis. Nor were the pyramids and temples as large as the Atlantean and Egyptian, Chinese, Bosnian, Serbian, Lebanese and Jewish structures.

All of these structures were constructed in extremely dense jungle vegetation. The climate was optimum for growing things and three crops of corn could easily be grown per year. Beans were planted as a companion crop to the corn, making it grow faster through the nitrogen produced by the leguminous beans, which means that the beans fixed/infused the growth enhancing properties of Nitrogen into the soil. And both crops helped to repel insect predator's specific to each of them. Fruit trees grew in the wild and were cultivated likewise, such as mango, papaya, coconuts, and bananas, as well as coffee.

What James was about to see was something with which he was very familiar. The Mayas used aquaculture to produce algae and fish and used the waste from the fish to fertilize their crops. The Algae was consumed for its nutritional value, which had a variety of nutrients and kept the bodies of the Mayan people alkalized. This allowed them to live in a state of radiant health, as well as all of the natural and unprocessed foods they consumed. Rarely did anyone experience sickness or disease; a vast array of jungle herbs and plants and trees were available for medicinal substances. They were in the form of tinctures, which included all elements of the herb; no synthesized ingredients like today's allopathic, pharmaceutical medicines.

James was also trained as a Doctor of Natural Medicine and knew herbal medicines were without iatrogenic (side effect) consequences. This revealed a vastly more evolved concept of healing than is known today, even though herbal healing is having a revival of sorts, in spite of it being frowned upon and belittled by prevailing allopathic system of medicine and the FDA!

Beyond the medicinal component of health, the men and women understood the emotional component in healing, as per Asclepius, in ancient Greece. In fact, emotions were considered the real causation of disease, especially the emotions of anger, fear, depression and loneliness. So for complete healing to occur, it was inherently understood that these issues had to be resolved. This was done through regressing a patient into a dreamlike state by a medicine man or woman, so that their emotions could be released and the subconscious mind reprogrammed into a state of fearlessness and happiness. With this achieved, long term healing and health was assured.

With the ability to go into dreamlike/trancelike and altered states of consciousness... researchers, scientists, priests, artists and musicians had a means to access celestial information stored throughout the cosmos in the electromagnetic field that pervades all creation, which was not available from Earthbound sources. This led to a vast infusion of knowledge and creativity into to the Mayan culture, where it flourished like few others that ever existed. They also created a calendar vastly more complex and accurate than the Gregorian calendar we use today.

It did not appear to James the Mayas used the tropical drink, Ayahuasca, as a means to go into higher dimensions to bring back medicinal treatment information like the Amazonian Indians. Certainly, the abilities of these Indians to go into higher dimensions and completely decode the structure of DNA and how to manipulate this DNA to heal were beyond anything done in the allopathic medical system today. In fact, the unwillingness of allopathic medicine to avail themselves to breakthrough treatments that can be accessed in higher dimension is certainly a shortcoming related to process. Regardless, it appeared to James the Mayas had the same abilities as the Amazonian Indians although they did not use the Ayahuasca hallucinogenic plant combinations!

It is believed, however, that the Mayans were involved in human sacrifice. While on the surface, this would seem to be true, in actuality what was occurring was an initiation to "attempted" immortality, akin to the Soruba Samadhi experience from Kriya Kundalini Yoga. So, while some of the initiates were killed during the so-called process of sacrifice, others literally transcended the state of death. Each initiate took an entire year of deep meditation to prepare for the impending day of reckoning, during the so-called sacrifice. Those who could suspend their breathing, blood flow and heart beat, were successful in achieving immortality of the body, which became basically a form of energy as opposed to flesh!

Eventually, the Maya's left Earth and returned to their star-born home. In fact, during his 1987 visit to the Mayan temples in the Yucatan Peninsula, James saw a picture of the God, Misol Ha, in a small spacecraft. Many archaeologists have posited that the population of the Mayan civilization outstripped their ability to grow enough food to feed all the people. This hypothesis is incorrect in that there was an ideal growing environment to grow crops and fruits. In fact, the Mayan's had an innate knowing of how important nature was to their well being and they knew how to manipulate the forces of nature to create more bountiful harvests than what would have been normally possible.

What was normally possible, in regard to what could be harvested, was already awesome and through the use of quartz crystals and other piezoelectric minerals such as topaz and tourmaline, the amounts of prana/electromagnetic energy, which accelerated plant growth, could be considerably increased. The use of holographic pyramids also amplified the prana intake of the plants and fruit trees, likewise, which accounted for the increased bounty derived from the trees and plants!

So once again, James learned much in his remote viewing experience; he allowed himself to be dazzled by the Maya's agriculture, pyramids and temples, spiritual practices, life extension and scientific prowess! *And yet*, James thought, so *many people still consider the Mayan's a primitive people. It is more likely the other way around!* James did not see either he or Ann having lifetimes in the Mayan lands. This does not mean they were not incarnated there, just that he did not receive anything related to the possibility!

But just when he was about to end this session of viewing, James saw the most amazing and intense experience where he was going through the "sacrifice"/Samadhi ritual. James could see himself and feel the pain of the wounds that were inflicted on him. He was able to slow his heartbeat and the resulting blood flow, but not in time to prevent his death. James saw he could suspend his breath, heartbeat, and blood flow while meditating, but failed to do so in the sacrifice ceremony. Maybe that is why James had become so fanatic in this lifetime about devoting so much time to Kriya Kundalini Pranayama and Samadhi so he would be ready to immortalize his body at the next opportunity!

| CHAPTER NINE

In his next remote viewing session, James saw remnants of the civilization of the destroyed continent of Atlantis also wound up in Peru and the Amazon Jungle, as well as Central America and Egypt. One strong indication of this is the amazing similarity between the multi-ton granite "L" shaped cornerstones in the Temple of the Sphinx in Giza Egypt and in a temple at Machu Pichu, in Peru. These are the only known temples that have these extremely heavy granite cornerstones in any type of structure. Actually, the same type of cornerstone was also used in Atlantis, but the evidence thereof is not extant at this time, since it is buried in the Atlantic Ocean.

What James viewed in Peru was a wonderful diversity. The most evolved civilization in Peru was the Incas, and like the Mayas, they predated significantly the time frames that are accepted by archaeologists! Like the Mayas, the Incas had regular visitation from extra terrestrial civilizations, which is indicated by the large landing strips in the Nazca Plains of Peru. These landing strips are still evident today from an aerial perspective. No place on Earth has such an extensive array of runways, which is indicative of this interaction from otherworld peoples, as well as other-evolved civilizations, which were regular occurrences. Even today, in Lake Titicaca (Quechua) located in the Andes on the border of Peru and Bolivia, the indigenous peoples regularly see spacecraft taking off from the submerged depths of this lake and also landing therein… to become submerged again.

There was also a temple complex in Moche, Peru, Cerro Chepen. It appears to predate Machu Pichu under the belief of current timelines, but actually the Machu Pichu ruins are much closer to 13,000 years old, rather than the several thousand-year timelines accepted by most archeologists. Anyway, this complex was built in hills and at a much lower elevation than Machu Pichu. There is also an enormous megalithic stone site located in Cuzco, Peru, which is many thousands of years old.

The topography of Peru is about as varied as any country in the world, ranging from beaches and tropical forests to deserts and mountains that extend above the tree line. Above the tree line, very few types of crops could be grown. Especially prolific was the growth rate that was sustained in the tropical regions and as a result, food was plentiful and again, as with the Mayan culture, the people knew the inherent importance and benefits from a close relationship with nature, especially the large trees in the tropical forests and the conifer forests in the mountains… the home of pine and other related trees.

The people who lived at or near tree line, developed tremendous lung capacity and were adept at breathing deeply. Thus, they were capable of extended breathing meditations, which allowed them to enter the exalted states of being at the level of theta/trance consciousness. With this advantage, they were able to enter into the realms of knowledge beyond that which exists in schools and texts. This was also true of the Amazonian Indians, who used Ayahuasca and other related hallucinogenic plants to access non-worldly information in higher dimensions than possible on Earth!

It was with this degree of consciousness the civilization was able to decode the structure of DNA, without the use of helium ion microscopes or other measuring devices. Some of the people achieved it with the psychotropic drug, Ayahuasca, but others were so deep in their meditative abilities they did not need any substance to enter the brainwaves levels of deep theta and upper delta states of consciousness! Additionally, it was with this knowledge that the Inca's used chanting to modify DNA to effectuate healings of physical maladies and disease in the body by stimulating the telomerase strands at the end of the DNA. The higher-level consciousness contributed to a state of great health that existed throughout a population that was rarely sick or diseased in the first place.

Also, because of the constant interaction with extra terrestrial civilizations, scientific knowledge and advanced spacecraft propulsion systems were well known and utilized throughout society. Additionally, power to run lights and devices in people's houses was available and transmitted without the use of wires or transformers. Light was created by activating quartz crystals with energy such as heat from the Sun, hot water, and fire. Geothermal magmatic devices also produced basically "free energy"/zero point energy

James was quite impressed with what he saw on the Nazca Plain in Peru, from the extensiveness thereof and the amount of aircraft and spacecraft that would have been using such a facility. Upon viewing this, James started observing a lifetime where he resided in the underwater base in Lake Titicaca. He was actually a pilot of an advanced propulsion system spacecraft, making regular flights between Lake Titicaca and the planet, Sirius B. The propulsion system of his craft was very similar and resembled the mercury iron propulsion systems detailed in the Indian Vedas.

This craft moved at the speed of light so the transit times where extremely shorter than the spacecraft used in the Apollo missions to the Moon. A self-supporting biosphere, which used hydroponics and aquaponics, was located inside the base of Lake Titicaca. So James directly experienced interplanetary visitation of other civilizations, as well as intra-planetary contact. The Lake Titicaca base, where even today spacecraft can be seen entering the lake and also existing there from, was probably very similar to those in The Devil's Triangle, Lake Erie, and the Bermuda Triangle, among others.

There are huge quartz crystal points in these areas, as well as Lake Titicaca and James saw these crystals were used as a power source. Yet they had another purpose, which was to create a vortex/wormhole that made interstellar travel much quicker, using the time warps therein! This also explains why planes and ship disappear from these areas, as they transit into higher dimensions.

It appears with the Incas, as well as the Mayas, the evolved inhabitants from these cultures eventually returned to their planets of origin, which accounts for their disappearance from Earth. This fact is little comprehended by today's archaeologists, who seem totally oblivious to extra terrestrial culture-visitation! In fact, it appears that many of these people did not actually leave, but began inhabiting the Earth's underground and underwater bases!

| CHAPTER TEN

THE INDIGENOUS PEOPLES OF AFRICA, NORTH AMERICA, AUSTRALIA AND NEW ZEALAND

With this large collective of people, there was such a deep connection to nature that it was an integral part of daily life. These peoples, by and large, were nomadic in nature, and literally lived off the land and migrated to different areas once resources began to be depleted or locate in a more temperate or cooler region to live more comfortably. But all these people knew how to use resources sustainably and nature was literally their religion and there was not much religious hierarchical structure.

The governmental structure was one guided by elders, which meant those with the most life experience were the ones responsible for making decisions for the tribes welfare! As James viewed these things, he kept thinking how much better this approach was than any governmental, religious, or corporate organization was normally run and administered!

It was understood that the Sun, being essential for living forms to exist on Earth, was the giver of all life and thus deific in its properties. The life force properties of the Sun were not only appreciated for the positive effect on crops and trees, it was further appreciated for its effect on maintaining health and vitality within the populations of these various cultures because of the pranic force/life force it would infuse in the human body. This understanding resulted in the overall population exhibiting vibrant health, where sickness was very rarely known.

It was interesting to James that these people had no fear of the Sun or skin cancer and he could see they did not cover their faces with the shade of a hat and they actually basked in the Sun, yet no one ever got skin cancer! If sickness did exist, witch doctors and medicine men and women used herbs and the clearing of negative emotions.

Resources, especially in regard to the killing of animals for food, were always gathered in a manner of sustainability. In the plains of the United States, buffalo existed in great numbers until the white settlers arrived and began not only to kill the buffalo for food, but likewise for sport. Buffalo herds were decimated; the American Indians handled the killing of deer, elk, and Moose in the same manner as buffalo. It was the basic concept of sustainability that extended to the killing of wild turkeys, pheasants, other small game and the catching of fish stocks.

Additionally, even though almost none of the American Indians settled in a stationary location, many of them had contact with extra terrestrial civilizations. Likewise, the Dogon Tribe in Africa interacted with cultures from Sirius and Nibiru. The Cherokee Tribe, in the central United States, also had contact with these advanced non-terrestrial civilizations, as did the Hopi's, Anasazi's and Navajo's in the southwest U.S., and myriad tribes from the Pacific Northwest U.S. Many of these extra terrestrial origins were indicated pictographically with images of space vehicles and/or by the extreme uniqueness of the people depicted in the art style prevailing at the time.

The ideas of sustainability by the indigenous peoples would be ignored and/or discarded as Europe, the U.S.A.

and even Asia and Africa, as developing civilizations were hell bent on industrialization. There was little or no thought for the long-term consequences of these actions in the quest to dominate and decimate nature, if not deliberately, at least from a state of ignorance. So today we deal with the residual effects from these consequences, and countries such as present day China, in their zeal to become a world power, completely ignored the senselessness of rapid and rampant development. The widespread pollution in China today is of epic proportions with immense negative health implications for the people living in this country!

Irrespective of this but actually related thereto, James started morphing into a lifetime with Ann as a Cherokee Indian. Ann was a brave and went out from time to time to hunt for food for the tribe. Hunting was not an individual pursuit but rather a group effort and everything that was killed was shared with the entire tribe. After an animal was killed, like a deer or buffalo, the hunters would always thank the animal and bless it for sharing itself as food for the tribe!

A strange twist… James was a squaw and Ann's wife, who bore two children. As well as taking care of the children, who could also be a communal effort, the squaw's were responsible for food preparation and cooking and the making of clothes and boots. This involved the preparation of grains to bake unleavened flat breads and preparing game and fish so they could be cooked. Neither of the roles of the males or females were considered superior to the other, but viewed as co-equal. So this was the operation of non-duality and Zeitgeist in a time frame very much before today, where these ideas were just beginning to gain traction and garner attention of the populace at large!

| CHAPTER ELEVEN

THE INDUSTRIAL REVOLUTION AND THE DECIMATION OF NATURE AND NATURAL RESOURCES

From a point wherein all past civilizations lived in awe and respect with the forces of nature, and especially the magnificent form of trees, by the time the industrial revolution came to Europe and then the U.S., this importance waned to the point that it was basically non-existent in the consciousness of humanity... or at least in the consciousness of the industry titans and big banks that were lending money to many enterprises.

This was something that James, a student of the esoteric sciences and ancient civilization, had an amazingly thorough perspective about since he was aware of all the preceding information and events listed in the previous chapters of this book, and because of his assiduous study of such. Therefore, by the time James reached an enlightened stage of his life in the beginning of the twenty first century, it was obvious that humanity could not continue much longer on its course of economic plunder of the Earth's resources and people!

It was also self-evident, at least to James, that any economic system—where money had no inherent value but was made from paper and backed only the various issuing government's promises to protect the value thereof—was unsustainable. Without being pegged to something of inherent value on Earth, the history of these currencies was a cycle of inevitably crashing and becoming valueless! This is exactly what happened in Great Britain in 1968 and Czechoslovakia in 1975. To this day, these countries, whose currencies become so highly devalued, still suffer the economic consequences.

Gold and Silver have always been used historically, to support currencies with an inherent value backing them! When this is not done it always causes great harm to the holders of these currencies, especially the population in general but with little consequences to the Central Bankers. James gleaned his perspective of this from the comprehensive articles related to this subject in *The American Free Press*, which is chock full of wise ways possible to govern countries!

The problem with blanket promises of a government's currencies, backed by private banks, like the Federal Reserve, as James learned, was that almost all of the world's governments in the twenty first century teetered on the edge of insolvency and bankruptcy. The underlying problem is the inability to live in a state of balance within the country's available resources, as opposed to what happens inherently within the operation and principles of Nature. James truly wondered, *how could people be oblivious to such a disastrous course of action? Furthermore, why would anyone use a currency system that sells securities to sustain its deficit spending; how can it be trusted by anyone?* James posited that these things were deliberately set in motion, so the rich people could get richer and the poor people, commensurately more impoverished; the actual chain of events operating within the world's countries clearly indicates this phenomenon!

The ancient societies understood at a fundamental or existential level that resources should be equally shared. They attained this basic understanding by realizing that plants and trees had long lived symbiotically in a Divine creation with proportional fractal principles, where all resources—Sun light, water, oxygen and nutrients—were used to their fullest extent without being hoarded or over depleted. If the large trees extracted too much water or too many nutrients from the ground, the other smaller trees and plants would be deprived of these resources and perish!

When a government does the same thing—using more resources than are sustainably available, be they natural resources or monetary revenues—inevitably the same thing will eventually happen. A few people like James and his wife, Ann, a few of their friends, and a scattering of other people and one or two politicians in the U.S., specifically Dennis Kucinich and Ron Paul, were keenly aware of this theory. They knew when the concepts of natural law—Nature itself—were ignored, disaster is always the ultimate result. But a vast sea of humanity still lives in ignorance of the impending crash of their currencies and the Earth itself. There is a growing awareness among the world's peoples about environmental degradation occurring on their planet, but obviously not sufficient concern to control the urge to over propagate the Earth with an excess of progeny!

James and Ann both knew these problems would have been considerably less significant if, in fact, people were in touch with the forces of Nature and trees. If people were in a situation where they had the ability and resources to support themselves through growing their own fruits, vegetables, beans and grains, they would not have been as vulnerable to monetary collapses or other conditions where the structure of society and the economic system could break down. A breakdown resulted from having no infrastructure in place to sustain the populace… a lack of fuel, electricity, and the transportation means to distribute life needs.

The United States personified an industrialized society, where a majority of the population lived in large, densely populated areas, bereft of land on which to cultivate personal gardens or have small commercial farming ventures—living off the land was extremely difficult, if not impossible. People living in high rise buildings and apartments could grow container gardens, vertical gardens in which containers were stacked vertically against a wall, or even maintain small aquaponics systems where they could grow some vegetables and raise some fish and have some small fruit trees on their apartment patios or balconies.

With aquaponics, fish such as Tilapia could be grown in a tank below the vegetables and then the water, containing fish excrement, pumped up to the vegetables to water and nitrify them. Some kind of power source would be necessary to run the pump for an aquaponics system, whether it is a portable or fixed solar electrical generating system. Other alternatives would be zero point energy systems based on magnetic or Tesla technology.

In the suburbs, conventional growing of vegetables and fruits was more easily achieved in the older residential areas because the residences tend to have larger lots than the newer residential developments. But living in the suburbs, even on a newer, smaller lot, was definitely preferable to being in a large metropolitan area, simply because it gave a person a better opportunity to grow more food and fruits. Still, too few people grasped the importance and necessity of living in the realms of Natural Law, at least in the perspective of James and Ann, viewed within the possibilities of natural disasters and other disturbances such as an economic collapse.

Whereas it seemed like ancient civilizations took nothing for granted and kept themselves more in a state of preparedness, it appeared to James and Ann that modern, twenty first century man, seemed to believe that there would be no interruption in their food supplies, building supplies, or electrical power grid. It was painfully obvious to James and Ann that this pervasive condition of complacency would surely cause problems when natural disasters caused things to break down and become non-functional, if they were not prepared with some sort of supply chain to replenish materials and food stocks.

James was especially concerned about the consequences: a series of strong electromagnetic pulses, via solar eruptions, coming from the Sun and blowing out the transformers in the electrical generation grid. Even Ann, who was no lover of firearms, realized they might become essential for survival if individuals or gangs got hungry and thirsty, and used force as a means to what they needed. At one time, James thought that if he took steps to stockpile food and water, then he would keep it for himself and Ann and not share it. James was appalled that people were so negligent in preparing for disasters and he should not be responsible for irresponsible people, who only lived for the moment with no regard for the future.

But finally, through the counsel of Ann and a friend, James realized that he and humanity would be best served if he shared his stores of food and water. James knew there were other people who were stockpiling necessities; he just wondered whether there were enough supplies to for all the unprepared people. James then thought of what Jesus did at the Sea of Galilee, where the master teacher multiplied the fish and bread into enough food to feed the multitudes of people. With this reminder, James realized that there could be another way to manifest enough food and supplies. The question was whether he would be able to do this for himself and other people, for that matter!.

Then the words of Jesus came to James in a flash one day, when Yeshua/Jesus said, "Greater works than these shall ye do also." In that moment James linked this Biblical quote with the insights he had learned from Dr. Lothar Schafer, a quantum chemist, in his book, *In Search of Divine Reality*. Therein, Dr. Schafer talks about there being all kinds of open space in the quantum field of consciousness where things could be created. The implications of this did not escape James' perception and he realized that we live in an infinite-possibility-Universe, not a place of scarcity. James considered the general consensus among Quantum Mechanics physicists that we quite literally create our own realities and experiences through our emotions, thoughts, activities, understanding and perception of things.

The inference of this knowledge is that the things we desire can be created out of seemingly nothing, even if this nothingness exists as empty space, waiting to be materialized into something tangible such as food, objects, or even a Zeitgeist civilization. James realized this idea is beyond the comprehension of most people, even though it has actual scientific backing, as well as the works of Jesus and Avatars in India, such as Sathya Sai Baba. Ann also reminded James of the video of Sathya Sai Baba they had watched many times; it was filled with instances where Baba manifested objects from seeming ethers/nothingness.

James found encouragement in the situation of potential disasters and the consequences to humanity from his own experiences with Nature and growing things, knowing trees and plants would find ways to survive, even in adverse situations! James remembered how trees and plants could quickly regenerate themselves after a forest or brush fire. He was amazed how consistently seemingly dead trees and plants regenerated themselves from their own roots, after being burned to the ground. And likewise, James noticed how seeds from plants quickly sprouted after rains followed a forest or brushfire. These were all thing people of ancient civilizations understood inherently, especially the nomadic people who lived off the land because their very survival depended on this relationship with Nature.

So Ann and James tried to ascertain how humans could apply these mechanisms of regeneration in nature to an adverse situation faced by humanity after some type of disaster. They knew trees and plants nourished each other and provided mutual cover for their plant neighbors. Could humans do the same? James and Ann knew there must be some mutual lessons to apply that came from Nature and the trees, plants and animals!

The first lesson James and Ann decided to apply to humans from the realms of Nature, were the concepts of cooperation and sharing resources, which were embodied in the concepts of the Zeitgeist movement, promulgated by the *Thrive* movie. According to the perceptions of James and Ann, the more challenging a situation confronted by humanity, the more important this concept was. Ann would often remind James, "Remember, James, the plants share their resources with each other without condition or stinginess."

The second lesson learned from Nature, applicable to humanity, was the concept of non-violence and peaceful coexistence. James recalled in particular, from his experiences in horticulture and agriculture, that large trees could easily take most of the nutrients and water from the smaller trees and plants, yet they only took what they needed, sharing with smaller plant friends so that they too could flourish/thrive!

The third concept James and Ann took from nature was the symbiotic relationship where trees and plants shared their food with animals and animals likewise would eliminate destructive insects from trees and plants and spread their seeds through their manures. And also, the various animals provided food for each other, through the predatory nature of sacrificing themselves, so another species was nourished and survived.

But the fourth, and most important example: tapping into the memories of the tree and plants and remembering how they had to adapt to mankind polluting and devastating much of the ecosphere on Earth. If this knowledge could be back engineered, solutions to pollution and deforestation could be enacted and employed to create the perfection of Aleph Kaf Aleph in the regeneration and the realization of the inherent perfection of all creation could be realized/re-realized!

So with these clear examples, it was rather obvious the concept of cooperation and sharing was an inherent part of nature and was something the so-called "superior humans" should emulate, likewise. James and Ann were quite familiar with the well-known English philosopher, John Locke and his fellow naturalists, who promoted similar concepts of natural law. The examples also proved the concepts of the Transcendentalists such as Emerson, Whitman and Thoreau, who embraced these theories while he lived in isolation in nature and wrote, *On Walden Pond*.

So with these inspirations, as well as those of the ancient civilizations that James and Ann had studied, they used the examples as guide posts to create the concepts for the impending Golden Age prophesized for humanity! There would be major hurdles to this task, including getting people to eliminate their phobias about the leaves and needles from trees, which many people considered were nothing more than a major nuisance and inconvenience, yet are actually the way Nature builds topsoil and increases soil fertility and productivity! Overcoming these obstacles would be necessary to instill and install the concepts of natural law into a working concept for humanity!

There was yet another factor which Ann pointed out to James, which would allow civilization on Earth to survive with little to no food to eat. "James," Ann exclaimed, "you have ignored the Breatharian concepts you and Dr. Newton discussed in Chapter Eleven of *A Map to Healing and Your Essential Divinity Through Theta Consciousness!*

"I did not really forget about this," James replied. "I know these Breathairian concepts of eating little or no food are within the realm of possibility and actually doable and I further know I can do it myself. Remember, Ann, the good Dr. Newton and myself learned that to pull this off it was almost imperative to have thoroughly mastered the Kriya Kundalini Pranayam Breath, Qui Gong and/or the Tai Chi Standing Meditation, since you need a significant amount of Prana/Chi/life force to sustain yourself without food. Do you recall articles in the *Journal of Metabolic Science* that stated at least twenty five percent of what nourishes the body comes from outside of the body itself? Peter Arthur Straubinger's documentary, *In the Beginning There was Light*, proves the body can exist without food or water and basically sustain itself vibrantly on this 'outside source,' namely Prana/chi/life force!"

"It is somewhat beyond my comprehension why people cannot summon the discipline to perform daily repetitions of this Pranayam breath," James continued, "so that they could reap the life changing rewards that come with mastering this discipline. I guess people would rather medicate themselves with beer and tranquilizers rather than improve and raise their consciousness and perception of things."

"All of these substances seem to relax people, but in such a way as many of them have little drive or motivation to take the steps to evolve to a higher level of consciousness and living," James explained. "We always talk about relaxing more so as to feel the pranic forces/life force/God force energies, yet this does not seem to happen in an alcoholic stupor or even after just a few glasses of wine! While it happens with

Cannabis, it may also over relax many users thereof and inhibit their productivity. I know this would be disputed by the Cannabis lobby and yet it has been proven that a person's reflexes and thought processes are slower than normal under the influence of Marijuana!"

"I know you have been extremely disappointed with the turnout at your classes when you teach Pranayam and other life changing disciplines," Ann sympathetically stated. "I know you know, James, eventually this will change as we transit into living in the fourth dimension, which hopefully will be sooner than later. But I also believe you and I already substantially live in this higher dimension, right James?"

James just looked goofily at Ann and said, "Duh, with all the Kriya Kundalini Pranayam we do and the Sanskrit mantras we recite, how could we not? Those who have the discipline to put in the work, reap the results and the corresponding rewards. Those who focus on sitting around and drinking a lot of beer, don't, because the drinker's are too relaxed, and thus unmotivated and mentally incapacitated, to wit! I am not saying such people are bad, just literally showing how they waste the tremendous potential they possess, as per "Hey Resh Chet," the 59th Name of God, from Exodus, which means connecting to the Light/God!"

"I guess that changes the whole game and means we are not up the creek without a paddle," Ann declared. James just nodded in agreement with a sardonic smile on his face!

| CHAPTER TWELVE

BRINGING PANTHEISM AND ZEITGEIST TO FRUITION BY ENSHRINING AND EMULATING NATURAL LAW

Clearly, there are at least two foremost obstacles to bringing Pantheism and Zeitgeist to fruition, from the circumspection that was the process which finally brought James and Ann to these realizations. They used the ideas and insights of each other to create a bigger perspective than they could have created by themselves and the mutual catalyst they shared with each other created something more than the sum of the singular parts of them as individuals. This in turn created a working prototype—a plan to implement Pantheism and Zeitgeist.

The first thing that would interfere with Zeitgeist and Pantheism were the incessant stream of wars in the last several centuries. These wars were always justified by demonizing a country or a people or a religion, through a continual barrage of propaganda to justify attacking a designated foe! James and Ann actually learned these wars were really instigated by the bankers, who made loans, which were saddled with interest, to governments to finance their aggressive forays… and by corporations making munitions, guns, tanks, helicopters, planes and missiles and other implements of war. The corporations that create materials of war came to be labeled the "industrial-military complex"

James was drafted into military service, as cannon fodder for the Vietnam War, and already hated war even before going to Vietnam as a soldier. But after actually being involved in many gruesome battles, James reached a point of radical opposition to all wars. He had seen too many of his friends maimed and killed in Vietnam and psychologically damaged with posttraumatic stress disorder (PTSD). Likewise, he had killed Vietnamese Army soldiers, Viet Cong and even probably innocent civilians. James told Ann one time, "If you have ever been in a war you should be convinced of the idiocy of such and the rampant destruction that occurs during a war or civil conflict/war, because you see way too many horrible things and atrocities that occur during battle. But in reality, you should be smart enough to figure this out without going into battle."

James continued, "The Vietnam War was manufactured; we attacked one of our own U.S. Navy vessels in the Gulf of Tonkin, just to rationalize entering into a conflict with North Vietnam. The entire Korean War could have been obviated if General MacArthur had been allowed to continue into North Korea during World War II. World War II could have been avoided if the U.S. had not imposed economic sanctions on Japan and if the international bankers had not funneled money to the Nazis; some of which was channeled through Prescott Bush, father of President George H. Bush. World War I was likewise manipulated into existence. There is no question, all wars are a tremendous waste of materials and lives, and it is as simple as that!"

The second thing that would interfere with bringing forth Zeitgeist/Pantheism/Natural Law as something that could be embraced by the general public was a general feeling among Christians, Moslems, and Jews, who resisted the idea that God is in everything and especially in Nature—essentially a Pantheistic concept. Certainly, the Christian faiths were most opposed to the idea of Pantheism as they viewed everything as segmented and separate and this even included the concept of God, as being some kind of distant, remote presence, reachable but yet separated from man. James, after writing *A Map to Healing and Your Essential Divinity Through Theta Consciousness* and *The Hidden Codes of God* with Dr. Robert Newton, and also reading Dr. Lothar Schafer's, *In Search of the Divine Possibilities*, knew Pantheism was a scientific reality and that God was in everything.

For James and Ann, all of life is accomplished through the atoms God created as building blocks of all creation, from the atomic level, to the human level... and on into the galactic level of manifestation. James knew this was intricately detailed in Valery P Kondratov's, *Geometry of a Uniform Field*. To the Christians, Moslems and Jews who could accept the findings of science, they might be inclined to reform existing beliefs, which were previously contrary and/or antagonistic to Pantheism, and Zeitgeist and Natural Law.

But there would be other "believers" of these faiths who would find this concept as too blatantly contrary to the *Bible*, *Torah*, and the *Koran*, and further proclaim that science has no place in religion. They might never accept Pantheism. In fact, these concepts are not contrary to all Jewish, Islamic and Christian scriptures; they were originally construed as such, but there would always be certain people who would cling to outmoded notions and knowledge they were previous taught and learned. They would disregard new information and concepts and higher spiritual knowledge as irrelevant, because it conflicts with what they perceived and learned as "truth."

A third thing impeding the progression into Zeitgeist, which really astonished James and Ann, was that there were a surprising amount of people who felt there was nothing wrong with a few people controlling vast amounts of wealth and resources. The people who held this view seemed to base their decision on the fact that someday they, too, could somehow become part of this very elite group of ultra rich people, or at least become moderately rich, without regard to how this might affect their friends and others and leave them behind to wallow in the throes poverty and the treadmill of middle class life. This premise indicated economic and social class distinctions were an accepted fact of societal structure, regardless of its dysfunction and negative implications for the masses of humanity!

Ann and James found the logic involved in such perceptions to be suspect and ignored basic statistics, which clearly indicated that although there are people who do break through the economic class barriers, by and large, this scenario never occurs for the vast majority of society. So apparently this indicates that most people who believe this upward economic mobility are living in a state of fantasy and/or delusion. Ann and James were not saying that economic mobility was impossible—just highly unlikely within the existing economic construct that is dependent on cheap labor so that the very rich can become immensely wealthy while the workers/masses linger in poverty with a poorly stacked deck—an oppressive system working against their best interests!

One of the major reasons for limited economic upward mobility of the populace at large is how the world and national banking systems work—or more matter-of-factly, how they do not work for the people at the lower end of the economic spectrum. In the United States of America, in 1917, the *Federal Reserve Act* was passed by Congress and signed by President Woodrow Wilson. When the Federal Reserve Banking system was being formulated, President Wilson was an ardent supporter thereof; he was unfortunately given inaccurate information on how this banking system would work. Sometime after he signed the *Federal Reserve Act* into law, Wilson realized he had made a huge mistake and even admitted such!

The practical result of the Federal Reserve System of banking was that Congress would no longer issue currency into the economic system. The Federal Reserve Banks, a private entity, became the issuers of money, even though the U.S. Department of the Treasury printed it, and the reserve actually charged interest on the money they ultimately loaned to The United States and various banks; the banks in turn charged even more interest than they paid as they further loaned money to people/companies who received loans. In essence, the banks were involved with usury, which violated the ecclesiastical concepts of Judaism, Christianity and Islam. This huge deception insured that much, if not all of the money created, was derived and backed by nothing of inherent value. At first, the U.S. Dollar was backed by gold and then by silver, however, later it became fractionalized, vapor currency, having no inherent value, when silver and gold currency backing of the currency abandoned by President Richard Nixon in 1971!!

The Constitution of the United States specifically delineated that Congress should be the issuer of money—not some private banking system. Ancient and modern history is replete with examples of fractionalized currencies becoming valueless, with always the same result, regardless which country the vapor/fractionalized currency has been used. So James and Ann reckoned that if currency was backed by gold or silver, it would always have some kind of value, since these metals were used in jewelry, manufacturing and in electrical circuits.

This was a good start to a sound banking, where the value of people's money could not be inflated or deflated, since every piece of currency would be backed by precious metal, in relation to its actual value. But to have true economic vitality, funds to expand business enterprises and for research and development, capital/money must be readily available. And if these funds were loaned without usury— without interest charges—then the possibility of an expanding economic vitality and productivity and wealth would be manifested prolifically. Ken Boshnack first proposed this idea in modern times through his proposal of *The Sovereignty Resolution.*

Also, James' friends Orion and Chad shared a lot information with him about crypto currencies, computer currencies, such as Bitcoin; a new kind of money and novel payment system. At first James was really leery of Bitcoin since there is volatility in the value thereof, with the worth going up and down frequently. James much preferred a currency with a stable value. But the long-term trend of Bitcoin was that of increasing value. So as James viewed this trend, as well as the fact that this currency could not be traced by governments and could not be taxed, the facts made Bitcoin more and more appealing to him and Ann. They both saw how Bitcoin could be protection against the inevitable crash of the U.S. Dollar and the Euro and extracting people, from the clutches and control of empowered governments and corporations!

Still another part of this economic equation was the concept of barter, which is basically the beneficial exchange of the goods or services of one party for those of another party. Although this medium of barter pre-dates the industrial age and even though there were people who dismissed this concept as impractical in modern times, James and Ann figured that if it worked in one age, with modern adaptations it certainly would be as successful in another time.

But then James watched a YouTube video where Michael Tellinger discussed an economy or a society based on no form of money, barter, trade or Bitcoin but on a natural order with no central authority. Tellinger called this economy UBANTU and the concept was that people in every city would band together, pool their talents and efforts, and share the fruits of their labors with their neighbors and even other cities. As he pointed out in the video, the method would be manifested by farmers, craftsmen, engineers and scientists, who would create this new economic system, since politicians have proven themselves incapable of doing so... or for that matter, creating anything else of any real value other than a lot of repressive and liberty squelching laws!

James had perceived the serious ineptitude of politicians many decades previously, about the time of the Vietnam War. And when Tellinger talked about how the banking system stops the flow of energy and prosperity from circulating throughout our World, it really hit a salient point for James and Ann! Tellinger's idea reminded James of how the trees, plants and animals existed in nature in a balanced state of cooperation and harmony!

Bringing things back into the perspective of Nature and Natural Law, if one species of tree in a forest proliferated to a point that it crowded out other varieties of trees, one species would become overly productive and result in an unbalanced state for the other plant and tree forms in Nature, and subsequently, the result would be an adverse affect on many of the surrounding wildlife/animals, many of which favor certain types of trees as habitat. And if a certain tree favored by certain animals became extinct, these particular animals would have to find a habitat in another area... possibly overtaxing the entire biosphere in the area where the animal migration occurred.

Similarly, when a corporation's business achieves the status of a monopoly or becomes overly large, its competitors are eliminated and wealth is concentrated in the hands of a very few people and corporations. This is exactly what exists today in the twenty first century. James and Ann realized it is this type of scenario that has exacerbated the inequality in the distribution of wealth between the world's countries and the important interstates within a country. So monopolies and quasi monopolies are always the culprit, which prevents a superior distribution of all known resources, irrespective of the economy of scale in a large monopoly that allows it to make a product at a cheaper price point.

James and Ann easily recognized any efficiency achieved by having one corporation control resource is more than negated by the disproportionate amount of control and money they acquire. Simply stated, the system does little more than lead to a level of greed that financially harms the populace at large; when one or a limited number of sources become extremely rich, the only natural alternative is that many people will be impoverished, at least relatively so!

Such are commodities exchanges, where people buy materials and bet the future price of these commodities will increase, and take "long position." When enough money is put behind a particular trade, the price is artificially inflated The net effect to the populace at large is that they have to pay higher prices for the things they consume and the devices they buy. This shift in economy continues to happen with some frequency, even when there is no real shortage of the commodity, other than the forces of trading. James and Ann wondered why this escaped the discernment of the masses; they were, after all, the very people most harmed by this state of business operations and unfair practices on Earth!

So in either case… hoarding resources, monopolizing production capacity, and manipulating the price of necessary commodities, the rich elite literally subjugates the masses in a state of poverty and/or unequal sharing of resources and wealth! Ann, considering all of this, asked James, "How do you stop this egregious greed factor in society? In the plant kingdom, there seems to be an inherent knowingness greed favors a few species, creates an inhospitable environment to plant diversity, and so is avoided. Can you understand that, James?"

James nodded yes and responded, "You are so completely correct, Ann!. The Creator manifested things in a balanced approach with fractal proportions that delineated how much of this tree and that tree and this plant and that plant would be distributed in Nature. The early civilizations I have studied, without exception, understood and lived by these precepts, at least until practicing the principles saw decline and deterioration. So all we have to do is learn and emulate the past to create the Zeitgeist and Natural Law that benefits the many instead of the "greedy few."

"Still, I am still searching," James continued, "for how we can convey this fundamental concept to those who, for whatever reason, are not so inclined to share the bounty, because in almost all cases, when shortages of commodities are claimed to exist, in fact, there is no real shortage at all! Originally, the viewpoint of science was to work within this natural construct and matrix of Nature and Natural Law! What the hell happened? Apparently, a very unbalanced civilization, from the perspective of wealth, and viewed without the parameters of Nature, has resulted in a worldwide state of unequal distribution of necessary resources and the resulting malfunctions, are seen as poverty for the masses."

"Wait a minute, James", Ann exclaimed. "What about those '72 Names of God' you are always studying and teaching and talking about. Isn't there a name that applies to this?" "Well," James replied, Mem Nun Daled (overcoming fears) would certainly put people in a state where they would not fear for their survival and thus be able to circumvent the emotions that create greed. Undoubtedly, Samesh Aleph Daled (the power of prosperity), would create a mindset that would help people circumvent the poverty consciousness that pervades society now and make people cleave unnecessarily to greed.

But Hey Resh Chet (connecting to the light/God) and Ayin Resh Yod (the certainty that God is always there and supporting us), would put people in a state of mind that should relegate greed to a non-factor status in the lives of people. Do you agree with this Ann… would this not go a long way to eliminating the greed mentality?"

"Yes," Ann replied, "I knew you would find something in those '72 Names of God.' Certainly, each name, hidden in Exodus in the *Torah*, is a gems therein—the one indispensible knowledge that certainly Jesus understood like no other student thereof."

"I agree," James responded. "Everything you would ever need to know is contained therein. I really wish I would have been exposed to those names decades ago. But once I was exposed to them—you know this only too well, Ann—I have been fanatical about studying them every day. The '72 Names of God' have allowed me to transcend my fears and find an inner tranquility and open my heart, as per 'Mem Nun Daled.' I am most grateful for the Kabbalah Center for bringing these names into the public domain.

"It is thus, self-evident," Ann exclaimed, "that these '72 Names of God' are an obvious means and protocol and practice to promote the concepts of Zeitgeist and Natural

Law and sharing. You and I know, James that world control, as exercised by the Illuminati, New World Order, and myriad other world controllers, in conjunction with the Zionists, Masons, Rothschild's, Rockefellers, and related ilk… even the Jesuits in The Roman Catholic Church, is pervasive throughout the Earth. Their agenda has always been based on keeping people "believing" there is a scarcity of resources, which subsequently promotes hoarding, and the escalation of prices for various commodities, sources of energy and electricity. It is the cause of all the wars, likewise! How many times have we discussed the reality that just by eliminating the feeding of grain to cattle, it would be quite possible to feed the entire world many times over and eliminate starvation of the World's people"

"You know I so agree with this," James replied, "and how could I not? There is little doubt in my mind organizations and the sub-organizations related to them: the Trilateral Commission, the Council on Foreign Affairs, the Bilderberger Group and the United Nations, have long been dauntless in painting a picture to perpetuate the concept of an inherently fallible and imperfect people here on Earth… a profound contradiction to the Divine templates we see on the atomic level of creation, the fractals geometries in Nature and in the great esoteric spiritual books such as *Science and Health with Key to the Scripture* by Mary Baker Eddy."

James' passion and wisdom were both quite clear as he continued his discussion, "And the divine qualities of humans are displayed in *The Emerald Tablets*, by Hermes Trismegistus, *The Pattern on the Trestleboard*, by Dr. Paul Foster Case and in *The 72 Names of God*, from Exodus 14, verses 19-21 and in *The*

Yoga Sutras, by Satguru Patanjali and in *Thirumandiram*, by Sat guru Thirumoolar."

"So when people feel they are imperfect and believe they must exhibit aggressive pursuit of food, energy and other resources," Ann added, "you get what we have now, a state of seeming imperfection and aggressive competition regarding the procurement of those very resources and the money to buy them."

"But when people realize the underlying perfection and abundance of everything at the atomic level and how this filters up to our locus," James replied, "then they are unshackled from this destructive, delusional ignorance and begin to act like the perfect loving beings they were created to be… in the image and likeness of God."

"Well," Ann said, "it is not like there are not ways to accelerate this process. Certainly there are ways to accomplish our goal through Christian Science, with the supporting messages in *Science and Health with Key to the Scripture*, which Mary Baker Eddy wrote over 150 years ago. Mrs. Eddy was the one person who kept hammering home the idea that we are in fact made in the perfect image and likeness of God, as depicted in the first chapter of Genesis. Mrs. Eddy was most adamant that we must literally "see ourselves" as this perfect reflection of God."

"How could I disagree?" James asked. "I am sure we used this very process to change ourselves considerably. But there is also the Silva Mind Control technique where you also see yourself in the state of perfection as we actually, but then again, this fits perfectly into Christian Science. You know, Ann, I really like the Swishing Technique used in Neuro

Linguistic Programming (NLP), where you "mentally" place a picture of something that you do not like in a frame, and then allow it to fade it away and mentally replace it with a new picture of what you do want materialized—the perfection that inherently exists. Certainly these are all valid ways to allow people to make mass changes, agreed, Ann?"

"Of course I agree," Ann emphatically stated, "but what if people resist the idea that they are perfect and tenaciously cling to the fallen sinner mode... the one we always see so pervasively held by many—probably all—Christians, other than Christian Scientists? And yet I remember clearly Mrs. Eddy speaking about how we—and this "we" is the critical point in this equation—must see all people as these perfect reflections of the Creator... and that by doing so we allow others and/or afford them the means by which they can evolve their consciousness to a more divine state of being and living."

"Agreed and then some," James replied, "but I'm sure you remember what I discovered about Theta Consciousness Reprogramming and Healing in my book with Dr. Robert Newton, *A Map to Healing and Your Essential Divinity Through Theta Consciousness*: to have a technique for changing ourselves and others as being the most comprehensive way of helping others evolve. In fact, Chapter Four is a detailed method, through human consciousness, to finally eliminate sickness and unhappiness, and the lack of wealth and resources that haunt our world. Among other things Dr. Newton and I wrote about is the first line of the names of God; at its core, it is suggestive of a successful Christian Science healing treatment protocol, although it was not specifically delineated as such by Mrs. Eddy. I am constantly reminded it has a hauntingly similar ring!"

"You mean the names, read right to left, which start with Vav Hey Vav (fixing the past and creating happiness) and Yod Lamed Yod (boosting your energy) and Samesh Yod Tet (which creates miracles)," Ann responded.

"That is correct, Ann, " James replied, "but there is more, as you know. The fourth name is Ayin Lamed Mem (eliminating negative thoughts), the fifth name is Mem Hey Shin, (which leads to healing), the sixth name is Lamed Lamed Hey (which comes from subconscious messages, which can come while awake, through dreams or lucid daydreaming), the seventh name is Aleph Kaf Aleph (restore things to their perfect state) and the eighth name is Kaf Hey Tav (defusing negative energy and stress). The entire method really is a progressive and systematic approach to healing that is extremely powerful; vastly more powerful than anything possessed by the prevailing allopathic system of medicine, hahahaha!"

James continued, "You can tell—or at least I can—that it will take something like this or NLP to change the perception of people so that they can manifest the perfect and optimum states of consciousness within themselves."

"I agree, Ann responded, "These protocols in *A Map to Healing*… are both powerful and effective. And beyond these, we need to get a whole different message dispensed to people in all the public media. The media outlets continue spewing forth misleading information and programming into the consciousness of people. That is why we have lack and greed;

it is actually something from peoples' unconscious, subconscious minds. That internet radio show you just started, *Real Conspiracies with Scientific and Spiritual Solutions*, has a powerful potential and way to do this—to actually put forth the positive and accurate templates/ideas that prompt people to realize just how empowered and prosperous and complete we are, as a people—all in the Divine presence of God."

"Agreed," James exclaimed rather vociferously. "I/we really need to get positive programming to a saturated mode of dissemination. The Illuminati cult, composed of the Bilderbergers, The Trilateral Commission, The Council on Foreign Relations, The United Nations, The Zionists, The Roman Catholic Church and the European monarchs, have long propagated and proliferated these false programs and ideals through their own PR and the public media, which they also effectively control through monopolies. The major media outlets are controlled by a very few large corporations. The "powers that be" have long promulgated and promoted this ongoing idea of limited resources and imminent shortages, when in reality the opposite is the real situation. Just go back to the way the trees in a forest or jungle share resources with the smaller trees and plants! The perfect template/model/pathway exists before our eyes and yet few have opened their hearts and minds to see it!"

"That is so correct, James," Ann replied, "you are so right about the tree example, and the claimed shortages of petroleum is another example of how easy it is to consistently spread disinformation and contrived shortages. Who dreamed up the lame ass idea that oil is the result of decomposing Dinosaurs? While some oil may have come from this, do you realize how many Dinosaurs would have had to live and die and decompose to have significant reserves of oil—probably many billions or trillions or quadrillions? I highly doubt there were ever that many dinosaurs and even if there were, they could have even decomposed into enough oil for us. Maybe we should check that out with Barney the Purple Dinosaur, hahahaha!"

"And this whole discussion does not include Hydrogen as a fuel, perpetual motion/zero energy generators, electricity created from the Ocean, including algae, tidal surges and coral electrical generation," James exclaimed. Nor does it include propulsion systems that individuals could use to provide themselves with "free energy." There are many kinds of magnetic technologies currently available, even a scientist in Japan who has a vehicle that uses magnetic power as a propulsion system, as opposed to an internal combustion engine. And of course there was John Keely, who produced perpetual energy using the notes of the musical scales. That was covered well in *The Journal of Sympathetic Vibratory Physics!*

"So, even if there were actually any kind of a shortage of petroleum and other fuels, the fact that these technologies have been deliberately suppressed by corporations and governments clearly indicates contrived shortages do not need to exist, Ann proclaimed!" Shortly after his death, the CIA confiscated all of Nikola Tesla's zero-point energy system research. This is just another indication of the deliberate suppression of things that would unshackle people from the power and gas producers! And the stench from those gas producers is the worst kind of malodorous flatulence, as you well know James!"

"You are right, "James responded, "It just goes to show you how stupid the Illuminati and their minions, think we really are! You and I, Ann, know that most oil is created through a biotic process where decomposing humic shale's reacts with hydrogen and actually create most oil deposits and this remains an unending process. Yet how many people in the general public even knows this?"

"Very few," Ann exclaimed, "and certainly not enough, from my perspective."

"And how many people know of the Keshe zero-energy generators or the Searle technology zero-energy generators or about the reality that Nikola Tesla proved he could literally pull electricity out of the atmosphere?" James questioned.

"Solar panels are really a positive step in the right direction of energy independence," Ann chimed in. "Those new solar panels that generate much more electricity than the older ones are especially intriguing, and so needed too. Yet too few people really realize that there are numerous 'non green' factors involved in the production of these panels which require many toxic substances in the process of their being manufactured. "

"You are very right about this," James replied, "so these magnetic energy generators, ocean tidal energy generating systems, and the Tesla energy accumulators are an overall superior solution, especially in areas that experience low sunlight days!"

Getting a little emotionally riled about issues over which there was so little control, James couldn't contain his next question. "What about the additional deception practiced by the pharmaceutical companies marketing drugs, shots and vaccines which cannot heal the cause of any malady, but actually create many iatrogenic conditions—many side effects from which people would not otherwise have to suffer!" James replied.

"And then we have the problem of toxic preservatives like mercury and formaldehyde and industrial toxins that are routinely placed in vaccines and shots, as a preservative," Ann answered.

Basically, whether we like it or not, the pharmaceutical companies charge us an exorbitant amount of money to take drugs and vaccines and shots that are toxic, create other problems to be treated and basically make us worse off than before we took anything," James emphatically stated. "All of these things are so greedy and disingenuous—it just boggles the mind. But luckily for us, there are alternatives and solutions for these situations. I would really love it if huge numbers of people stopped using these pharmaceuticals so the companies themselves would be bankrupted and we would regain the privilege to use natural and mental remedies to heal ourselves in conjunction with nature. as opposed to synthesized pharmaceutical medicines."

"You know," Ann countered, "the mental and emotional healing protocols we have used, as per Christian Science treatments via Christian Science Practitioners and NLP and Dr. Newton's and your, *A Map to Healing…*" and Louise L. Hay's, *You Can Heal Your Life*, are so powerful and effective I portend there is no longer a valid need for pharmaceutical companies, other than to feed the ignorance of a world of people and the government and insurance company mandates that basically require the their use."

"What a racket—what an obnoxious monopoly laced with the worst form of greed," James asserted. "This crap needs to end and the more we make these things known, such as on my internet radio show, *Real Conspiracies...* the sooner things will turn around and greed will end and people will be healthier and no longer be charged exorbitant prices for medical care and fuel for their vehicles."

"Remember too, Ann," James continued, "the product, ASEA, is a stabilized redox solution, which can completely rejuvenate the body—literally reverse the aging process, creating a cellular regeneration. I feel this product is able to attract more prana/life force/electromagnetic energy into the body, which is really what stimulates the cellular rejuvenation. But just as important, if not more, is the fact that somehow, someway, ASEA causes a shift in the brain triggering an entrainment in theta trance/divine consciousness. There may indeed by DNA reprogramming, which actually is a computer code as per Dr. Yockey's book, *Information Theory, Evolution and The Origins of Life.*

"Actually," James continued, "the mental effects of this particular product goes way beyond the brain. If you assess it closely, you will recognize it as a shift in consciousness, which allows for the access of information stored in the unified field. This is called "Akashic Knowledge" in the Hindu *Vedas* and *Upanishads* and "celestial knowledge" in *The Yoga Sutras* by Sat guru, Patanjali, and also discussed in Dr. Hurtak's, *The Keys of Enoch.* Essentially, it enables people to not only acquire unlimited knowledge from the electrical field and cosmic computer related thereto, but to also access an endless connection to incredible creativity."

"Wait a minute!" Ann exclaimed, rather excitedly, "Isn't ASEA the product that can quickly eliminate cancer from the human body?"

"Yes it is," James stated, "and it completely eliminates cancer, unlike chemotherapy and radiation, which just makes the cancer cells go into hiding, only to return later! And it does so at such a significantly lower price, it is ridiculous; yet it is not FDA approved for this purpose!"

"But it is a given we know how to eliminate cancer using the Richway Bio-mat, likewise, "Ann responded." We both know of numerous cases where cancer has literally been cooked out of the body, raising the body temperature significantly for an hour or two at a time!"

"Correctamundo," James agreed, "and there is also significant pain relief using Bio-mat as well as with ASEA. So by using these things to create and reclaim health, the vast amounts of hard-earned money that allopathic medicine and pharmaceutical drugs extract from the populace in general, could be eliminated and we could use our money for better purposes, rather than for 'half ass' therapies and drugs that only partially work—at best! Of course, I have no idea just how many people would agree with me on this, but I could really give a flying Shiite, since we both know our statements are factually correct!"

"The technology for the Bio-mat is simple yet effective," James continued. "Patients sit on, lay down or sleep on a mat filled with amethyst quartz or amethyst and black tourmaline, which emits a strong piezoelectric field of energy. That energy transmits infrared rays and negative ions, to achieve healing and mood elevation. The benefit come in when the amethyst and black tourmaline become energized with the electrical source that comes with the mat; the energy and healing effects are then multiplied. I am comforted only in knowing you share my frustration that once again, like other natural healing alternatives, Bio-Mat is not FDA approved for anything except pain relief!"

"Have we saved the world yet, James?" Ann laughed as she asked a question that focused on their shared goal in life.

"Certainly we have gained insights into many problems yet I am sure there are more things that would improve things to Aleph Kaf Aleph, in our quest to "restore things to their perfect state," James replied. "But for sure, this will so drastically improve things as to cause a cataclysmic shift in consciousness and to create heaven on Earth. Undoubtedly… undeniably, things will become so much better that people will be in a state of confusion, just trying to catch up with the perceptual and operational changes that will occur, as the Earth is finally prepared and able to transit into the fourth dimensional state of consciousness and energy."

"And," Ann responded, "there will be peace on Earth as all people's needs and survival will be ensured and you can smile and say, 'Sayonara to greed,' because what we suggest actually manifests most of the concepts in the movie, *Thrive* and *Avatar*!"

"And yet there are still more things we have to deal with," James exclaimed, "and we must never forget UBANTU!

| CHAPTER THIRTEEN

FINDING MORE PIECES OF THE ZEITGEIST/NATURAL LAW PIE AND PUZZLE AND HOW THIS FITS INTO ROMANCE!

James could hardly contain his excitement as he exclaimed, "You know, Ann, we really have considered many things that will remediate conditions on Earth and restore it to Aleph Kaf Aleph perfection, and yet we still have more things to consider. Certainly the global warming notices have been misconstrued and misunderstood in light of the actual facts related thereto. It appears, in a great many cases where scientists have blamed greenhouse gases/carbon emissions for global warming, they were paid to come to these conclusions and deliberately steered in this direction, also. But you and I, Ann, had an experience in Atlantis where we uncovered something similar to this… and what did we get but to be imprisoned indefinitely without a trial!"

"What do you mean by that," Anne queried?

"Well," James replied, I never told you about that past lifetime experience I had when I looked into the ancient cultures that are rarely talked about or even known about. However, I also mean just what I said and more about global warming. Now, it is undeniable that global temperatures have been rising, but why that happens and the mechanisms related thereto, have been obscured by scientists ignorant of the big picture or, Aleph Nun Yod, the 37th Name of God, which translates, 'to grasp the big picture behind our obstacles.' And even beyond that, did you know, Ann, that every Ice Age in the history of the Earth was preceded by a rapid rise in global temperatures and then bam! We get thrust into an ice age."

"Wow," Anne responded, "I did not know that and it kind of changes the whole perspective of this global warming scenario. However, I do know, James, there are at least three factors contributing to this global warming and they have been discussed in numerous articles in the *American Free Press*. One of the reasons for this warming trend has to do with the Earth shifting back and forth on its axis over a period of about nine years, always between 21 and 23 degrees, and in one position the Earth gets cooler and while in another position it gets hotter."

"Still another reason is increased solar eruption/plasma ejections on the Sun—more than a normal or average amount," Ann continued. "And this seems to be related to an increased amount of hydrogen available as fuel for the Sun; this is the third reason I was alluding to. It is because the Sun is transiting through an area that has increased space dust and contains more hydrogen than normal. This was discussed in a blog downloaded by Dr. Newton entitled, *Removing the Shackles*, which can be viewed on Dr. Robert Newton's Blog and *Real Conspiracies with Scientific and Spiritual Solutions*, on Facebook."

"Yeah, I saw that article and also read those *American Free Press* articles and it all makes perfect sense," James exclaimed!" You have these do-gooder idiots like former senator and vice president, Ozone Al Gore, running around telling people that we are going to burn up and will experience massive flooding… when the Ice Age scenario is more likely what we will have to deal with. You remember, Dr. Iben Browning knew this more than 20 years ago and talked about this in a video, Climate *and the Affairs of Man*. I guess ole Ozone Al was to busy writing his pseudo treatise, *An Inconvenient Truth*, to view this video. I really wish he would pull his head out of his ass and search for unprejudiced scientific truth rather than so-called scientific babble. Beyond that, if we go into an Ice Age, while the winter temperatures will be colder, the summer temperatures will actually rise! An Ice Age also means a shorter growing season, which impacts the amount of food that can be produced to feed humanity."

Ann then added, "What you say seems to be true, James. It would appear that this whole global warming/carbon emissions myth is nothing more than a ploy for The United Nations to impose carbon taxes with which to fund their Tower of Babel world government scheme."

"Agreed," James replied, "you mean the same U.N. where money seems to disappear into black holes or into the ethers, never to be accounted for, Ann? I have a very strong feeling those missing billions of dollars were most likely just siphoned off into Illuminati/Zionist secret, off-book bank accounts. I remember someone reported in the *American Free Press* newspaper more than fifty trillion dollars was siphoned into these off-book accounts. According to the article, not all of the tapped money came from the U.N. but some of it was traced back to income taxes collected in various countries… illegally imposed income taxes, to wit; meaning there are really no true legal powers of collection, other than through the coercive act of imposing liens on people's bank accounts and real estate!"

"But getting back to that *Removing the Shackles* blog; did you read, Ann, where the Sun is getting hotter and is actually a catalyzing factor that will raise the Earth's vibration to the fourth dimension? Apparently the atoms in the surrounding atomic field will spin faster, create a higher electrical potential, and thus more energy will surround us. We can't forget this fourth dimension makes everything easier for us to accomplish, or that each successively higher dimension contains more complex geometries underpinning it, as per Valery Kondratov's, *Geometries of a Uniform Field*, since there is more energy/Prana/Chi/life force available for us to access!"

"Yes," Ann replied, "and that just gives us another example of "intelligent design" as a controlling factor in our Universe. It indicates a Creator who has an immensely larger understanding of things than a bunch of human scientists or thinkers/philosophers, right James?"

"Correctamundo!" James blurted out, "It does become self-evident when viewed from an impartial perspective! And further Ann, did you see the Sun getting hotter also causes the Earth to be pushed further away from the Sun, thus alleviating our global warming? This is another indication of 'intelligent design, right?"

"Yes on both counts!" Ann declared. "Everything has been set up in the Universe on a very precise operating system; very possibly within those computer codes we have been talking about as being a binary-pairs computer code, which seems to be morphing to quaternary-pairs computer code, which amazingly enough is just like our DNA!"

"Oh," James replied, "you must be referring to the recent discovery that this quaternary-pairs computer code was found in the cancer virus. That discovery just corroborates information to the claim we will be adding strands of DNA to our bodies. Of course the claim by some people, none of them scientists by the way, is ultimately we are going to have twelve-strand DNA! I never thought the concept as credible, and even somewhat bombastic and unnecessary, since there are innumerable combinations of DNA available in just a binary-pairs DNA. But I suppose it is certainly possible… eventually, a twelve-strand DNA may be part of our genetic makeup in the distant future!"

"But the fact that quaternary pairs DNA have been discovered in the cancer virus would certainly make one think that the same thing was occurring in human DNA or will be happening in the near future," James continued. "This could have many implications, including the possibility that electrical circuits/acupuncture meridians could exist in the human body, and provide circuits/pathways for far more Prana/Chi/life force to be circulated throughout the form that delineates us from other people and things. In such a higher state of being infused with Prana, the real energy essence of the human body would be more apparent."

"Additionally," James explained to a very attentive Ann, "it would mean that the body could function in such a state of Divine perfection that sickness and disease would be non-existent. And transcending death and trans-morphing into an immortal light-body would certainly be within the realm of the possible… even the probable!"

After a few quiet, somewhat introspective moments, Ann then asked James, "What about the possibility of an increased capacity to store and retrieve information from a more highly developed brain-computer? Likewise, would not this doubling of DNA strands also enhance the brain, James?"

James answered without hesitation as he replied, "That is certainly very possible, in fact our brains, which area are already super computers because of the vast amounts of information they can store, even when we are not consciously aware of what it encodes, could possibly attain aspects of a hyper dimensional computer. Thus it might even store things in the alternate realities when we go to a sleep/dream state of consciousness. Think of the possibilities if it might also store things from higher dimensions we have not even visited."

"Good God!" Ann exclaimed rather forcefully. "The implications are rather…well, really, completely staggering. I mean we would approach Godlike status, having so much knowledge we could access at will. But would this increase a person's creativity or psychic insights or even result in more devout spiritual impulses? You know, James, the big rage now is everyone is talking about Pineal gland activation, and it being a pathway to higher levels of consciousness akin to super consciousness or Divine Mind, as Mary Baker Eddy revealed in *Science and Health with Key to the Scriptures*.

"Yes," James replied, "I agree with all of what you have shared with me, except that I still do not see that dinky Pineal gland in our brains being significant beyond the fact it releases chemicals within the brain, which allow an alchemical process to occur that transports us into super consciousness, theta consciousness, Akashic consciousness, Divine Mind, God Consciousness. Once this alchemical reaction occurs, which means there is a process, result, or shift to a vastly higher consciousness that happens in an incredibly short span, we are in a closer link with The Creator, at the very worst."

James barely took time for another breath before he continued, "And eventually, as we are perceptually able to assimilate the necessary background foundation, we establish a direct link with God, as things were originally created. It might be the Pineal gland is like a "cosmic antenna" that allows us to receive psychic impulses and also receive insights and information from other realms/dimensions!"

"James, James, James!" Ann exclaimed excitedly. "What you have just shared with me is so incredibly insightful and liberating. The way you described all of it is so clear and makes so much sense, especially when you relate all of this to nature and how trees communicate with each other!"

"I agree," James replied. "And no one has ever found a brain in a tree or plant, and yet we know from such books as *The Secret Life of Plants*, by Peter Tompkins, there is sentience, where our sensory organs make us aware of certain things, and sufficient recent research, which shows trees and plants do actually communicate with each other through their roots and branches! There are also some recordings from plants that indicate music being created there from!"

"Well," Ann responded, "We both agree this mental telepathy between plants is clearly revealed in the movie, *Avatar*. And just as you and Dr. Newton wrote about this in *The Hidden Codes of God* and *A Map to Healing and Your Essential*

Divinity Through Theta Consciousness, it is now very clear humans can communicate with each other and trees and animals with virtually no verbal interface but by projecting pictures and images of things. Remember that book we both read, *Kinship With all Life*? The author was J. Allen Boone and he wrote of communicating with all sorts of animals... even a fly and a rock? Do you think the brain-computer is an integral part of this telepathic communication, James?"

"I know you are just asking me a rhetorical question here because you already know both I and Dr. Newton have done enough research to prove that while the brain displays certain brainwaves, which indicate theta consciousness, and levels of super consciousness, Akashic consciousness, Divine Mind and/or God Consciousness, it is just not capable of creating these links to exalted consciousness. This is just what we shared in *A Map to Healing*.... that physicist, Jay Lakhani, declared no part of the brain has been found which indicates a designated place wherein consciousness can be detected. So, likewise, it is quite likely neither the trees nor we need a brain to access consciousness and the higher levels therein!" I also remember that amazing *Kinship With all Life* book. I am still caught with how truly amazing is the level of telepathy Boone exhibited in that book!"

With a heightened curiosity that matched that of James, Ann queried, "Then what do you and Dr. Newton consider is going on in this higher consciousness equation?"

"As far as we can discern and ascertain," James' voice changed to a rather tutorial tone, "there seems to be an alignment with the electrical field of the atoms and the atomic force generated by these atoms that allows transference of communication between person to person, person to animal, person to trees and person to Divine Mind/Akashic Mind, etc."

"Those chemicals mentioned that exist deep within the pineal gland may help in eliciting this higher consciousness as they interact with the atoms in some way," James continued. "Dr. Newton and I know that Kriya Kundalini Pranayam, the Tai Chi Standing Meditation, the Backflow Meditation and Qui Gong also transport a person to the highest possible levels of consciousness and they might stimulate the pineal gland in a corresponding manner. So quite possibly trees are as intelligent and creative as man, and as in the case with dolphins, possibly even more so. Certainly both trees and dolphins are at least as divine as humans, if not more so, since they do not have a need for war and always seem to naturally express their inherently divine nature!"

"Ann, Did I ever tell you about the two studies, where Dr. Newton and I discovered that atoms stimulated in one place transferred that stimulation to atoms billions of miles away? It kind of blew our minds while concurrently made us grateful to find these studies."

"Wow," Ann replied, "That blows my mind, too; what you are saying could also lead us to conclude atoms likewise have a sentience, and intelligence and higher consciousness! I am sure you and Dr. Newton would have no problem with the idea that trees and dolphins are our teachers, right James?"

"Duh!" James replied, "but you know, Baby, we have engaged in so much time pontificating here we have really not engaged in embracing each other, except for holding hands.

Here we are, in this incredible forest, thick with trees and being the presence of these exalted tree and plants, and it has filled me with gratitude and relaxation. I think I need to get a blanket and we need to dance ourselves into a very private and remote spot in this forest and begin an excursion into the land of sexual pleasure and elation."

James continued, "I really would rather be caressing you, Ann, than talking about what we have, even though we are dealing with serious concerns. The solutions to the world's problems could literally be contained in the world of romance and sexuality. In those sexual realms is a transcendent energy that takes us to heaven and into an embrace with our Creator. That is the place wherein trees and plants routinely reside. So, let's cut the jive and turn up the vibe and make like a tree and be real free and begin our cosmic dance with our Creator, which we should do sooner rather than later."

"We need to intertwine our branches like the trees often do!" Ann exclaimed. "Oh, and by the way Baby, what sparked you into a state of waxing poetic?"

"Duh, Ann," James replied, "Obviously it was you and the trees. I cannot really think of any two things more Divine."

"Good God, James," Ann responded, "You really know how to make a woman melt into your arms."

"Does that include getting you to meld with me in this enchanted forest?" James queried. "I think we need to dance our way thereto in a slow and deliberate manner!"

Ann just looked at James with "far away eyes" in the most sultry manner and James knew that the bonding process between them had already begun… and then some!

So James responded in kind to Ann with his own sultry looks, starring back into her eyes and wrapping both of his hands around hers. This initiated an electrical circuit between them, but beyond the aspects of the circuit, it just felt very special and sublimely intense. As James and Ann got older, the more they realized the importance of building the sexual energies in a patient manner. As was explained in the Tantric and Taoist texts they had studied, the deliberateness of the process would always lead to rewards at the culmination of the sexual conjoining when their orgasms were unleashed.

So after a considerable time, possibly twenty minutes or so, James stood up and lifted Ann and wrapped both his arms around her. He then began to slowly dance with Ann to a remote spot in the forest, playing a Sanskrit mantra/prayer on a CD that he had just recorded and saved to his cell phone. James really surprised Ann with this sacred and yet sensual music, since he had not told her he had completed the CD and was now just playing it.

"Oh, Baby," Ann cooed, "that Gayatri Mantra is so ethereal and spiritual!"

"But is it sexual, too, Baby?" James probed.

"I am not sure that it is inherently sexual, per se," Ann replied, "but it certainly is making me relax and we know that relaxing allows us to absorb more sexual energies, which are most certainly intensified Prana/Chi/life force energy from The Creator!"

"Then sexual, it is!" James exclaimed as he laughed out loud. As James and Ann were passionately dancing and slowly turning in circles, James looked deeply into Ann's eyes and then began to kiss her lightly. He remembered from his very first girlfriend, for many women, this softer initial approach to kissing was less abrupt and allowed his woman to kind of melt into his arms in a less confrontational manner, creating a trust between them that nurtured the energy they attracted, created and amplified between themselves.

As their dance progressed, James started kissing Ann much longer, deeper and far more intensely. He let it be a gradual process, in which he focused his thoughts on his eventual sexual orgasm with Ann, but also remained in the moment of things. He found they each basked in and absorbed the energies they created and, in that present moment, lived solely in the ecstasy there from.

Ann responded as James desired, cooing, on and on, "Baby James, this is so divine and beyond sublime. The more we extend this dance, and the sexual dance to come, the more intense and exciting these things become!"

It was obvious the couple had a long-standing, healthy relationship as they bantered in fun and frolic. "Baby," James whispered in Ann's ear, "I concur and I am not thinking about what will be cumming/coming because my body is already humming."

"Humming be I too," Ann whispered in kind, yet I might be close to cumming!"

As the couple danced in the direction of their secluded spot in the forest, several times they almost tripped and fell, yet due to their deft maneuvering, somehow they remained upright. Eventually, they reached a remote spot in the forest they had visited before. James spread their blanket on some grass and he began to remove Ann's top, pants and shoes and his own pants, shirt and shoes. Then he pulled Ann down on top of himself, and as he reclined backward Ann landed on top of him and laughingly used him as a cushion. James and Ann intertwined with each other, descending into a level of deeper intimacy. Their joy flooded forth as the full contact embrace and skin merging activated a galvanic response with corresponding electrical circuits that attracted a deeper energy of love. The more the electricity flowed, the more the couple relaxed, which allowed the ecstasy of the energy of love to be embraced and experienced between them.

In such a state, spontaneous creativity became second nature; both James and Ann intuitively knew how to pleasure the other without having to use a routine or specific protocol. After removing Ann's socks, James sucked Ann's toes and massaged the Reflexology points on her feet. That this was unconventional move was irrelevant to James since he was only focused on giving Ann as much pleasure as possible. It was apparent to James he was succeeding as he listened to Ann's moans and groans of delight. The Reflexology points, which are akin to acupuncture meridians, activated Prana/Chi energy circuits in Ann's body.

Instinctively, James assumed a spooning position with Ann and eschewed penetration with his penis. He just relaxed instinctively and wrapped his arms around her, creating more contact between them. Ann really enjoyed being enveloped in this manner and let James know when she said, "I feel like you are using your branches to surround and embrace me."

James' laugh was hearty as he replied, "That is the idea, and precisely what I had in mind. The power of the examples shared in Nature is just too instructive and omnipresent to ignore. Many times you and I have seen tree branches cross and embrace other tree's branches, and we felt a deeper sense of the electrical interchange being shared! And I bet when the tree branches rub into each other it is like foreplay, to wit!"

James then rolled Ann on her other side with her left shoulder facing upward, lay behind her and spooned himself against her body again. This position allowed them both to be more receptive to each other's energy, even without the physical joining of penis and vagina. Ann then shared, "Well I cannot really disagree with your observations about the tree branches… in fact at this very moment I feel the energy and electricity building between us. I do not know where you came up with this offbeat sexual variation, but it sure could go a long way toward controlling Earth's prolific birthrates right now, especially if people practiced Tantric Sex, of which this is a variation!"

James then interjected, "I was thinking that myself and amazingly enough, I feel the energy between us building to a crescendo, and that we will both have intense non-penetration orgasms."

For about twenty minutes Ann and James remained in the spooned position; they fondled and relaxed into a deeper level and found their breathing become very deep and slow. In fact, James' prophetic statements soon were simultaneous orgasms of such energy intensity, both he and Ann screamed out loud for a long time.

Even after their orgasms, the energy exchange between the pair continued as they entered an even of deeper state of relaxation. The ensuing exhilaration, even though subtle, was sublime beyond all words; very few words were exchanged between Ann and James as the energy that linked them together, sexually, established a telepathy where they both vividly read the other's most intimate thoughts. For several hours they lingered, intertwined in each other and the forest, basking in the amazing energy field they had created.

James would remember and savor this experience with Ann, as shortly thereafter she became gravely ill. It really perplexed James that Ann eschewed his herbal knowledge and tried to regain her health through the allopathic model of medicine prevalent today. The medicine the doctor's used only worsened the continual vaginal bleeding that Ann experienced. With a cayenne pepper tincture, a natural medicine made by grinding the pepper with vodka in a blender, James knew he could stop the internal hemorrhaging from Ann's fibroid tumor. However, Ann continued to get weaker over the next month, but on the day that Ann was to pass into another dimension and leave her body behind, James intuitively knew she had reached the end in this incarnation, although a large part of him had serious difficulty acknowledging—or rather, accepting it!

Ann's last few hours were excruciatingly painful for her and equally so for James; as an empath he felt what was going on inside other people. As much as James intensely disliked hospitals, he actually begged Ann to allow him to take her to a hospital so they could put her on a morphine drip to ease her pain. Ann refused this course of action replying, "I do not want to be on life support and I do not trust the hospital to follow my wishes. And so it was… in the evening of that sad, fateful day, Ann passed on to another dimension!

James was as stoic as he could summon himself to be, but entered periods of having tears unconsciously fill his eyes, facing the reality Ann would no longer be with him on Earth… at least in her existing body. However, he could feel the essence of her presence resurrected, as she communicated telepathically with him, he was able to let go of his grief! One thing about Ann's death that soothed James somewhat was when her consciousness left her body; he observed Ann physically leaving through the top of her head, as all Kriya Yoga yogini's are taught to do. The purpose of this "leaving" is to depart the body through the Crown Chakra, so as to have a better connection with God when transiting into the higher dimension of death.

A short time after her death, Ann telepathically told James, "I remain interested and will watch and communicate with you as you continue your quest to establish Zeitgeist on Earth and seek immortality for your existing body. I think you can pull it off, but you must stop wasting Prana/Chi/life force when you get so upset about things not going as you want them." The part of a wife that engages with a spouse obviously remained as James heard her further comment, "It is retaining that extra potentially wasted energy that will allow you to "pull off" that immortality gig! You can no longer allow that Prana/Chi/life force energy to leak from your body through releasing anger! Namaste, my sweet James, and may you continually bask in the light as per Hey Resh Chet, the 59th Name of God!" James was touched by Ann's reference to the Hebrew translation, "Divine umbilical cord to remove spiritual darkness."

Ann left James with much to ponder, but he allowed his immediate thoughts to flow, *At least I have my own personal angel in heaven. I hope there are a lot of trees there, Ann! I really have savored our union we had on Earth. I learned so damn much from you. Namaste, my love, until we meet again and unite in the higher dimensions of heaven!*

| ABOUT THE AUTHOR

Dr. Robert J. Newton has lived his life much in the manner he writes... with a quest to surround himself with the highest level knowledge in the myriad areas that ensure we live rich, full lives. His education has been extensive, ranging from Speech and English at Cal State Fullerton, to a Juris Doctorate from American College of Law, and many certifications in alternative healing. He formalized his career in Naturopathic Medicine as a graduate of Clayton School of Natural Healing.

Newton has lived to serve others; operating an award-winning landscape and design company for many years, as a Christian Science healer for two decades, and more recently as an author, speaker and life and relationship coach. Yoga, Metaphysics, Spiritual Sciences, Natural Healing, World Religions, Ancient Hermetic teachings... this philosopher and champion for the world has tapped into the roots of spirituality, sexuality, life and love—all with the purpose to enlighten those with a common desire to utilize multiple methods and strategies to approach life more effectively, creatively, radiantly and with great abundance.

Today, Dr. Newton lives his life looking forward... honoring the love and the beliefs he shared with his wife, and writing more novels to plant a "What if" seed in the minds of his readers.

Thank you for reading Beyond the Mists of Time.

Gaining exposure as an independent author, I rely mostly on word-of-mouth, so if you have the time and inclination, please consider leaving a short review wherever you can.

| CONTACT INFORMATION

Amazon Author Central
http://www.amazon.com/Dr.-Robert-J.-Newton-J.D.-N.D./e/B0080CCFCQ

Author Website
http://www.drrobertnewton.com/
http://www.drrobertnewton.com/books.html
http://www.greatmotivationaltalks.com/

Beyond the Bounds of Earth Publishing
  - Entertainment and Education

Social Media

LinkedIn: https://www.linkedin.com/pub/dr-robert-newton/52/31/666

Twitter: https://twitter.com/DrRobertJNewton

Facebook: https://www.facebook.com/pages/Dr-Robert-Newton/184989068280581?fref=ts

YouTube:
https://www.youtube.com/channel/UCBwmCVMWwMVPJBxKW9gmQmA/videos
https://www.youtube.com/watch?v=MujJqRn5w08&feature=youtu.be&a

Other Books by the Author

The Hidden Codes of God
CreateSpace eStore: https://www.createspace.com/5388561

Amazon: http://www.amazon.com/Hidden-Codes-God-Journey-Dimensions/dp/0996137106/

A Map to Healing and Your Essential Divinity Through Theta
Consciousness: The Physics of the Immortal "Light Body"
by Dr. Robert J. Newton J.D. N.D. (Mar 28, 2012)
http://www.amazon.com/dp/B007SDHOL0 (Kindle)
http://www.amazon.com/dp/145254445X (Print)

Pathways to God: Experiencing the Energies of the Living God in Your
Everyday Life
by Dr. Robert Newton April 6, 2012
http://www.amazon.com/Pathways-God-Experiencing-Energies-Everyday-ebook/dp/B00844NSIK   (Kindle)
http://www.amazon.com/dp/1452546398 (Print)

NOTES

45416201R00100

Made in the USA
Charleston, SC
20 August 2015